Mornings With Mary

(A Rosary Prayer Book)

Mary Kloska

En Route Books and Media, LLC
Saint Louis, MO 63109

D0887047

Make the time

En Route Books and Media, LLC
5705 Rhodes Avenue
St. Louis, MO 63109

Cover credit: Mary Kloska

ISBN-13: 978-1-956715-00-2

The Fifteen Promises of Mary to Those Who Recite the Rosary

1.) Whoever shall faithfully serve me by the recitation of the rosary, shall receive signal graces.

2.) I promise my special protection and the greatest graces to all those who shall recite the rosary.

3.) The rosary shall be a powerful armor against hell, it will destroy vice, decrease sin, and defeat heresies.

4.) It will cause virtue and good works to flourish; it will obtain for souls the abundant mercy of God; it will withdraw the heart of men from the love of the world and its vanities, and will lift them to the desire of eternal things. Oh, that souls would sanctify themselves by this means.

5.) The soul which recommends itself to me by the recitation of the rosary, shall not perish.

6.) Whoever shall recite the rosary devoutly, applying himself to the consideration of its sacred mysteries shall never be conquered by misfortune. God will not chastise him in His justice, he shall not die an unprovided death; if he be just he shall remain in the grace of God, and become worthy of eternal life.

7.) Whoever shall have a true devotion for the rosary shall not die without the sacraments of the Church.

8.) Those who are faithful to recite the rosary shall have during their life and at their death the light of God and the plenitude of His graces; at the moment of death they shall participate in the merits of the saints in paradise.

9.) I shall deliver from purgatory those who have been devoted to the rosary.

10.) The faithful children of the rosary shall merit a high degree of glory in heaven.

11.) You shall obtain all you ask of me by the recitation of the rosary.

12.) All those who propagate the holy rosary shall be aided by me in their necessities.

13.) I have obtained from my Divine Son that all the advocates of the rosary shall have for intercessors the entire celestial court during their life and at the hour of death.

14.) All who recite the rosary are my son, and brothers of my only son Jesus Christ.

15.) Devotion of my rosary is a great sign of predestination.

(Given to St. Dominic and Blessed Alan) Imprimatur: Patrick J. Hayes DD Archbishop of New York)

Table of Contents

Chapter 1

The Beginning Prayers

Sign of the Cross

"In the Name of the Father and of the Son and of the Holy Spirit –Amen."

Morning Offering

O Jesus, in union with Your most Precious Blood poured out on the Cross and offered in every Mass, I offer you today my prayers, works, joys, sorrows and sufferings for the praise of Your Holy Name and all the desires of Your Sacred Heart; in reparation for sin, for the conversion of sinners, the union of all Christians (for all of the intentions of my heart) and for our final union with You in heaven. Amen.

Marian Consecration

My Queen and My Mother, I give myself entirely to Thee;
And in order to show devotion to Thee I consecrate to Thee this day: my eyes, my ears, my mouth, my heart, my entire self without reserve;
Wherefore good Mother, as I am Thy Own,
keep me and guard me as Thy property and possession. Amen.

Prayer of Jabez

" (Jabez prayed,) 'Oh that You would bless me indeed, and enlarge my territory, that Your hand would be with me and that You would keep me from evil, that I may not cause pain!' –*So God granted him what he requested...*" (1 Chronicles 4:9-10)

Angelus

The Angel of the Lord declared to Mary:
And she conceived by the Holy Spirit.

Hail Mary, full of grace, the Lord is with thee; blessed art thou among women and blessed is the fruit of thy womb, Jesus. Holy Mary, Mother of God, pray for us sinners, now and at the hour of our death. Amen.

Behold the handmaiden of the Lord:
Let it be it done unto me according to Thy word.

Hail Mary...

And the Word was made Flesh:
And dwelt among us.

Hail Mary...

Pray for us, O Holy Mother of God, that we may be made worthy of the promises of Christ.

Let us pray:

Pour forth, we beseech Thee, O Lord, Thy grace into our hearts; that we, to whom the incarnation of Christ, Thy Son, was made known by the message of an angel, may by His Passion and Cross be brought to the glory of His Resurrection, through the same Christ Our Lord. Amen.

Regina Caeli (Latin)

V. Regina caeli, laetare, alleluia.

R. Quia quem meruisti portare, alleluia.

V. Resurrexit, sicut dixit, alleluia.

R. Ora pro nobis Deum, alleluia.

V. Gaude et laetare, Virgo Maria, alleluia.

R. Quia surrexit Dominus vere, alleluia.

Oremus.

Deus, qui per resurrectionem Filii tui, Domini nostri Iesu Christi, mundum laetificare dignatus es: praesta, quaesumus; ut per eius Genetricem Virginem Mariam, perpetuae capiamus gaudia vitae. Per eundem Christum Dominum nostrum.

Regina Caeli (English)

V. Queen of Heaven, rejoice, alleluia.

R. For He whom you did merit to bear, alleluia.

V. Has risen, as he said, alleluia.

R. Pray for us to God, alleluia.

V. Rejoice and be glad, O Virgin Mary, alleluia.

R. For the Lord has truly risen, alleluia.

Let us pray.

O God, who gave joy to the world through the resurrection of Thy Son, our Lord Jesus Christ, grant we beseech Thee, that through the intercession of the Virgin Mary, His Mother, we may obtain the joys of everlasting life. Through the same Christ our Lord. Amen.

Chapter 2

Rosary Prayers

<u>Apostle's Creed</u>

I believe in God, the Father Almighty, Creator of heaven and earth and in Jesus Christ, His only Son, our Lord; Who was conceived by the Holy Spirit, born of the Virgin Mary, suffered under Pontius Pilate, was crucified, died, and was buried, He descended into hell; and on the third day He arose again from the dead; He ascended into Heaven, and is sitteth at the right hand of God, the Father Almighty, from thence He shall come to judge the living and the dead. I believe in the Holy Spirit, the Holy Catholic Church, the communion of saints, the forgiveness of sins, the resurrection of the body, and life everlasting. Amen.

<u>Our Father</u>

Our Father, Who art in Heaven, hallowed be Thy name; Thy Kingdom come, Thy will be done on earth as it is in Heaven. Give us this day our daily bread; and forgive us our trespasses as we forgive those who trespass against us; and lead us not into temptation, but deliver us from evil. Amen.

<u>Hail Mary</u>

Hail Mary, full of grace, the Lord is with thee, blessed art thou amongst women and blessed is the fruit of thy womb, Jesus. Holy Mary Mother of God, pray for us sinners now and at the hour of our death. Amen.

<u>Hail Mary in Russian</u>

Радуйся Мария, Благодати полная, Господь съ Тобою благословенна Ты между женами, и благословень плодь чрева Твоего Іисус.

Святая Мария, Матерь Божия, моли о насъ грешныхъ ныне и въ часъ смерти нашей. Аминь.

<u>A phonetic pronunciation in English:</u>

Rah-dooie-seeyah Mah-ree-yah, blah-go-dahtee pohl-nah-yah Gohs-pohd st-boy-oo blah-go-sloh-vienna tee mez-doo z-nah-mee, ee blah-go-sloh-vee-en p'load ch-ray-vah t'vo-yeh-goh Yee-soos.

S'vee-yah-tah-yah Mah-ree-yah, Mah-t'yair Boh'zee'yah moh-lees oh nahs, gresh-neekh, neen-yah ee v'chahss smair-tee nah-shay-yeh. Ameen.)

<u>Hail Mary in Polish</u>

Zdrowaś Maryjo, łaski pełna, Pan z Tobą, błogosławionaś Ty między niewiastami, i błogosławiony owoc żywota Twojego, Jezus. Święta Maryjo, Matko Boża, módl się za name grzesznymi teraz i w godzinę śmierci naszej. Amen

<u>Hail Mary in Spanish</u>

Dios te salve, María, Llena eres de gracia, el Señor es contigo. Bendita tú eres entre todas las mujeres, y bendito es el fruto de tu vientre, Jesús. Santa María, Madre de Dios, ruega por nosotros, pecadores, ahora y en la hora de nuestra muerte. Amen

Hail Mary in Italian

Ave Maria, piena di grazia, il Signore è con te. Tu sei benedetta fra le donne e benedetto è il frutto del tuo seno, Gesù. Santa Maria, Madre di Dio, prega per noi peccatori, adesso e nell'ora della nostra morte. Amen.

Hail Mary in Latin

Ave Maria, gratia plena Dominus tecum benedicta tu in mulieribus, et benedictus fructus ventris tui, Jesus. Sancta Maria mater Dei, ora pro nobis peccatoribus, nunc et in hora mortis nostrae. Amen.

Glory Be

Glory be to the Father, the Son, and the Holy Spirit. As it was in the beginning is now and ever shall be, world without end. Amen.

Glory Be in Latin

Gloria Patri, et Filio, et Spiritui Sancto, Sicut erat in principio, et nunc, et semper, et in saecula saeculorum. Amen.

Fatima Prayer

O my Jesus, Forgive us our sins. Save us from the fires of hell. Lead all souls to heaven, and help especially those who are most in need of thy mercy. Amen.

Come Holy Spirit

Come Holy Spirit, Come by the means of the powerful intercession of the Immaculate Heart of Mary, Thy well-beloved Spouse.

Mysteries of the Rosary

Joyful Mystery of the Rosary

(*Monday and Saturday*)

> **First Mystery:** The Annunciation of the Lord to Mary
> **Second Mystery:** The Visitation of Mary to Elizabeth
> **Third Mystery:** The Birth of Baby Jesus in Bethlehem
> **Fourth Mystery:** The Presentation of our Lord Jesus in the Temple
> **Fifth Mystery:** Finding of the Child Jesus in the Temple

Sorrowful Mystery of the Rosary

(*Tuesday and Friday*)

> **First Mystery:** The Agony of Jesus in the Garden
> **Second Mystery:** The Scourging at the Pillar
> **Third Mystery:** The Crowning with Thorns
> **Fourth Mystery:** The Carrying of the Cross
> **Fifth Mystery:** The Crucifixion and Death of our Lord

Luminous Mystery of the Rosary

(Thursday)

First Mystery: The Baptism of Jesus in the Jordan

Second Mystery: The Wedding at Cana

Third Mystery: The Proclamation of the Kingdom *(the Preaching of Jesus, the Call to Repentance and the Healing Miracles)*

Fourth Mystery: The Transfiguration

Fifth Mystery: The Institution of the Eucharist as a Foreshadowing of the Cross

Glorious Mystery of the Rosary

(Wednesday and Sunday)

First Mystery: The Resurrection of Jesus Christ

Second Mystery: The Ascension of Jesus to Heaven

Third Mystery: The Descent of the Holy Spirit upon the Apostles at Pentecost

Fourth Mystery: The Assumption of Mary into Heaven

Fifth Mystery: The Coronation of Mary as Queen of Heaven and Earth

Chapter 3

Prayers at the End of the Rosary

Hail Holy Queen

Hail Holy Queen, Mother of Mercy, our life our sweetness and our hope. To thee do we cry, poor banished children of Eve; To thee do we send up our sighs, mourning and weeping in this valley of tears. Turn then, most gracious advocate, thine eyes of mercy toward us and after this our exile show unto us the blessed fruit of thy womb, Jesus. O clement, O loving, O sweet Virgin Mary!

V: Pray for us, O Holy Mother of God

R: That we may be made worthy of the promises of Christ.

LET US PRAY

O God, whose only begotten Son, by His life, death, and resurrection, has purchased for us the rewards of eternal salvation. Grant, we beseech Thee, that while meditating on these mysteries of the most holy Rosary of the Blessed Virgin Mary, that we may imitate what they contain and obtain what they promise, through Christ our Lord. Amen.

Memorare

Remember, O most gracious Virgin Mary that never was it known that anyone who fled to Thy protection, implored Thy help, or sought Thy intercession was left unaided. Inspired by this confidence, we fly unto Thee, O Virgin of virgins, our Mother. To Thee do we come; before Thee we stand, sinful and sorrowful. O Mother of the Word Incarnate, despise not our petitions, but in Thy mercy, hear and answer us. Amen.

Prayer to St. Joseph

Oh, St. Joseph, whose protection is so great, so strong, so prompt before the throne of God. I place in you all my interests and desires. Oh, St. Joseph, do assist me by your powerful intercession, and obtain for me from your divine Son all spiritual blessings, through Jesus Christ, our Lord. So that, having engaged here below your heavenly power, I may offer my thanksgiving and homage to the most loving of Fathers.

Oh, St. Joseph, I never weary of contemplating you, and Jesus asleep in your arms; I dare not approach while He reposes near your heart. Press Him in my name and kiss His fine head for me and ask him to return the Kiss when I draw my dying breath. St. Joseph, Patron of departing souls - Pray for me.

Prayer to St. Joseph Against Demons

O Saint Joseph, Terror of Demons, cast thy solemn gaze upon the devil and all his minions, and protect us with thy mighty staff.

Thou fled through the night to avoid the devil's wicked designs; now with the power of God, smite the demons as they flee from thee!

Grant special protection, we pray, for children and the unborn, for our families and relationships, work and ministries, homes and possessions, for persecuted Christians, priests and the dying.

By God's grace, no demon dares approach while thou art near, so we beg of thee, Saint Joseph, always be near to us!

Prayer to St. Michael (Short Form)

St. Michael, Gabriel, Raphael, Seraphim and Cherubim, Thrones and Dominions, Virtues, Powers Principalities, Archangels and Guardian Angels, defend us in battle. Be our protection against the wickedness and snares of the Devil. May God rebuke him, we humbly pray, and do thou, O Princes of the heavenly hosts, by the divine power of God, thrust into hell Satan, and all the evil spirits, who prowl about the world seeking the ruin of souls. Amen.

Prayer to St. Michael (Long Form)

One day, after celebrating Mass, the aged Pope Leo XIII was in conference with the Cardinals when suddenly he sank to the floor in a deep swoon. Physicians who hastened to his side could find no trace of his pulse and feared that he had expired. However, after a short interval the Holy Father regained consciousness and exclaimed with great emotion: "Oh, what a horrible picture I have been permitted to see!"

He had been shown a vision of evil spirits who had been released from Hell and their efforts to destroy the Church. But in the midst of the horror the archangel St. Michael appeared and cast Satan and his legions into the abyss of hell. Soon afterwards Pope Leo XIII composed the following prayer to Saint Michael, which is the original version:

"O Glorious Prince of the heavenly host, St. Michael the Archangel, defend us in the battle and in the terrible warfare that we are waging against the principalities and powers, against the rulers of this world of darkness, against the evil spirits. Come to the aid of man, whom Almighty God created immortal, made in His own image and likeness, and redeemed at a great price from the tyranny of Satan.

"Fight this day the battle of the Lord, together with the holy angels, as already thou hast fought the leader of the proud angels, Lucifer, and his apostate host, who were powerless to resist thee, nor was there place for them any longer in Heaven. That cruel, ancient serpent, who is called the devil or Satan who seduces the whole world, was cast into the abyss with his angels. Behold, this primeval enemy and slayer of men has taken courage. Transformed into an angel of light, he wanders about with all the multitude of wicked spirits, invading the earth in order to blot out the name of God and of His Christ, to seize upon, slay and cast into eternal perdition souls destined for the crown of eternal glory. This wicked dragon pours out, as a most impure flood, the venom of his malice on men of depraved mind and corrupt heart, the spirit of lying, of impiety, of blasphemy, and the pestilent breath of impurity, and of every vice and iniquity.

"These most crafty enemies have filled and inebriated with gall and bitterness the Church, the spouse of the immaculate Lamb, and have laid impious hands on her most sacred possessions. In the

Holy Place itself, where the See of Holy Peter and the Chair of Truth has been set up as the light of the world, they have raised the throne of their abominable impiety, with the iniquitous design that when the Pastor has been struck, the sheep may be scattered.

"Arise then, O invincible Prince, bring help against the attacks of the lost spirits to the people of God, and give them the victory. They venerate thee as their protector and patron; in thee holy Church glories as her defense against the malicious power of hell; to thee has God entrusted the souls of men to be established in heavenly beatitude. Oh, pray to the God of peace that He may put Satan under our feet, so far conquered that he may no longer be able to hold men in captivity and harm the Church. Offer our prayers in the sight of the Most High, so that they may quickly find mercy in the sight of the Lord; and vanquishing the dragon, the ancient serpent, who is the devil and Satan, do thou again make him captive in the abyss, that he may no longer seduce the nations. Amen.

V. Behold the Cross of the Lord; be scattered ye hostile powers.

R. The Lion of the tribe of Judah has conquered, the root of David.

V. Let Thy mercies be upon us, O Lord.

R. As we have hoped in Thee.

V. O Lord, hear my prayer.

R. And let my cry come unto Thee.

Let us pray.

O God, the Father of our Lord Jesus Christ, we call upon Thy holy Name, and as supplicants, we implore Thy clemency, that by the intercession of Mary, ever Virgin Immaculate and our Mother, and of the glorious St. Michael the Archangel, Thou wouldst deign to help us against Satan and all the other unclean spirits who wander about the world for the injury of the human race and the ruin of souls. Amen."

Angel of God

Angels of God, our guardians dear, to whom God's love commits us here, ever this day be at our sides, to light and guard, to rule, to protect, to defend, to enlighten and to guide. Amen.

Prayers for the Souls Who Have Died

Eternal rest grant unto them, O Lord, and let Your perpetual light shine upon them. May the souls of the faithful departed, through the mercy of God, rest in peace. Amen.

St. Gertrude's Prayer for Souls in Purgatory

Eternal Father, I offer to You the Most Precious Blood of Thy Divine Son, Jesus, in union with the Masses said throughout the world, for all the holy souls in purgatory, for sinners everywhere, those in the universal church, within my own home and within my own family. Amen.

St. Patrick's Breastplate Prayer

St. Patrick's Breastplate is a popular prayer attributed to one of Ireland's most beloved patron saints. According to tradition, St. Patrick wrote it in 433 A.D. for divine protection before successfully converting the Irish King Leoghaire and his subjects from paganism to Christianity. (The term breastplate refers to a piece of armor worn in battle.)

I arise today
Through a mighty strength, the invocation of the Trinity,
Through belief in the Threeness,
Through confession of the Oneness
of the Creator of creation.
I arise today
Through the strength of Christ's birth with His baptism,
Through the strength of His crucifixion with His burial,
Through the strength of His resurrection with His ascension,
Through the strength of His descent for the judgment of doom.
I arise today
Through the strength of the love of cherubim,
In the obedience of angels,
In the service of archangels,
In the hope of resurrection to meet with reward,
In the prayers of patriarchs,
In the predictions of prophets,
In the preaching of apostles,
In the faith of confessors,

In the innocence of holy virgins,
In the deeds of righteous men.
I arise today, through
The strength of heaven,
The light of the sun,
The radiance of the moon,
The splendor of fire,
The speed of lightning,
The swiftness of wind,
The depth of the sea,
The stability of the earth,
The firmness of rock.
I arise today, through
God's strength to pilot me,
God's might to uphold me,
God's wisdom to guide me,
God's eye to look before me,
God's ear to hear me,
God's word to speak for me,
God's hand to guard me,
God's shield to protect me,
God's host to save me
From snares of devils,
From temptation of vices,
From everyone who shall wish me ill,
afar and near.
I summon today
All these powers between me and those evils,

Against every cruel and merciless power
that may oppose my body and soul,
Against incantations of false prophets,
Against black laws of pagandom,
Against false laws of heretics,
Against craft of idolatry,
Against spells of witches and smiths, wizards, Satanists and
warlords,
Against every knowledge that corrupts man's body and soul;
Jesus Christ to shield me today
Against poison, against burning, against choking and
suffocating, against destruction and accidents, against
pestilence, infestation and plague;
Against drowning, against wounding, against sickness and
calumny, against jealousy, competition, blocking, division,
against rash or false judgment, against vanity, selfishness and
pride, against anger and lust, against dishonesty and betrayal,
against denial, abandonment, rejection, indifference and
unfaithfulness, and against every evil that could come against
me,
So that there may come to me an abundance of reward.
Jesus Christ be with me,
Jesus Christ before me,
Jesus Christ behind me,
Jesus Christ in me,
Jesus Christ beneath me,
Jesus Christ above me,
Jesus Christ on my right,

Jesus Christ on my left,

Jesus Christ when I lie down,

Jesus Christ when I sit down,

Jesus Christ when I arise,

Jesus Christ in the heart of every man who thinks of me,

Jesus Christ in the mouth of everyone who speaks of me,

Jesus Christ in every eye that sees me,

Jesus Christ in every ear that hears me.

[Note that people sometimes pray a shorter version of this prayer just with these 15 lines about Christ above. The conclusion follows below.]

I arise today

Through a mighty strength, the invocation of the Trinity,

Through belief in the Threeness,

Through confession of the Oneness

of the Creator of creation.

Chapter 4

Monday Prayers –to the Holy Spirit and Souls in Purgatory

Come, Holy Spirit, Come!

Come, Holy Spirit, come!
And from your celestial home
Shed a ray of light divine!

Come, Father of the poor!
Come, source of all our store!
Come, within our bosoms shine.

You, of comforters the best;
You, the soul's most welcome guest;
Sweet refreshment here below;

In our labor, rest most sweet;
Grateful coolness in the heat;
Solace in the midst of woe.

O most blessed Light divine,
Shine within these hearts of Thine,
And our inmost being fill!

Where you are not, we have naught,
Nothing good in deed or thought,
Nothing free from taint of ill.

Heal our wounds, our strength renew;
On our dryness pour your dew;
Wash the stains of guilt away:

Bend the stubborn heart and will;
Melt the frozen, warm the chill;
Guide the steps that go astray.

On the faithful, who adore
And confess you, evermore
In your sevenfold gift descend:

Give them virtue's sure reward;
Give them your salvation, Lord;
Give them joys that never end.

Consecration to the Holy Spirit

On my knees before the great multitude of heavenly witnesses, I offer myself soul and body to You, Eternal Spirit of God. I adore the brightness of your purity, the unerring keenness of your justice, and the might of your love. You are the Strength and Light of my soul. In You I live and move and I am. I desire never to grieve you by unfaithfulness to grace, and I pray with all my heart to be kept from the smallest sin against you. Mercifully guard my every thought and grant that I may always watch for your light and listen to your voice and follow your gracious inspirations. I cling to you and give myself to you and ask you by your compassion to watch over me in my weakness. Holding the pierced Feet of Jesus and looking at His Five Wounds and trusting in His Precious Blood and adoring His opened Side and stricken Heart, I implore you Adorable Spirit, helper of my infirmity, so to keep me in your grace that I may never sin against you. Give me grace O Holy Spirit, Spirit of the Father and the Son, to say to you always and everywhere, "Speak Lord, for your servant is listening." Amen.

Prayers for the Gifts of the Holy Spirit

O Lord Jesus Christ Who, before ascending into heaven did promise to send the Holy Spirit to finish Your work in the souls of Your Apostles and Disciples, deign to grant the same Holy Spirit to me that He may perfect in my soul, the work of Your grace and Your love. Grant me the Spirit of Wisdom that I may despise the perishable things of this world and aspire only after the things that are eternal, the Spirit of Understanding to enlighten my mind with the light of Your divine truth, the Spirit of Counsel that I may ever choose the surest way of pleasing God and gaining heaven, the Spirit of Fortitude that I may bear my cross with You and that I may overcome with courage all the obstacles that oppose my salvation, the Spirit of Knowledge that I may know God and know myself and grow perfect in the science of the Saints, the Spirit of Piety that I may find the service of God sweet and amiable, and the Spirit of Fear that I may be filled with a loving reverence towards

God and may dread in any way to displease Him. Mark me, dear Lord with the sign of Your true disciples, and animate me in all things with Your Spirit. Amen

Litany of the Holy Spirit

Lord, have mercy on us, Christ have mercy on us. Lord, have mercy on us.

Father all powerful, Have mercy on us.

Jesus, Eternal Son of the Father, Redeemer of the world, Save us.

Spirit of the Father and the Son, boundless Life of both, Sanctify us.

Holy Trinity, Hear us.

Holy Spirit, Who proceedest from the Father and the Son, *Enter our hearts.*

Holy Spirit, Who art equal to the Father and the Son, *Enter our hearts.*

Promise of God the Father, *Have mercy on us.*

Ray of heavenly light, *Have mercy on us.*

Author of all good, *Have mercy on us.*

Source of heavenly water, *Have mercy on us.*

Consuming Fire, *Have mercy on us.*

Ardent Charity, *Have mercy on us.*

Spiritual Unction, *Have mercy on us.*

Spirit of love and truth, *Have mercy on us.*

Spirit of wisdom and understanding, *Have mercy on us.*

Spirit of counsel and fortitude, *Have mercy on us.*

Spirit of knowledge and piety, *Have mercy on us.*
Spirit of the fear of the Lord, *Have mercy on us.*
Spirit of grace and prayer, *Have mercy on us.*
Spirit of peace and meekness, *Have mercy on us.*
Spirit of modesty and innocence, *Have mercy on us.*
Holy Spirit, the Comforter, *Have mercy on us.*
Holy Spirit, the Sanctifier, *Have mercy on us.*
Holy Spirit, Who governest the Church, *Have mercy on us.*
Gift of God the Most High, *Have mercy on us.*
Spirit Who fillest the universe, *Have mercy on us.*
Spirit of the adoption of the children of God, *Have mercy on us.*

Holy Spirit, Inspire us with horror of sin.
Holy Spirit, Come and renew the face of the earth.
Holy Spirit, Shed Thy Light into our souls.
Holy Spirit, Engrave Thy law in our hearts.
Holy Spirit, Inflame us with the flame of Thy love.
Holy Spirit, Open to us the treasures of Thy graces.
Holy Spirit, Teach us to pray well.
Holy Spirit, Enlighten us with Thy heavenly inspirations.
Holy Spirit, Lead us in the way of salvation.
Holy Spirit, Grant us the only necessary knowledge.
Holy Spirit, Inspire in us the practice of good.
Holy Spirit, Grant us the merits of all virtues.
Holy Spirit, Make us persevere in justice.
Holy Spirit, Be our everlasting reward.

Lamb of God, Who takest away the sins of the world, *Send us Thy Holy Spirit.*

Lamb of God, Who takest away the sins of the world, *Pour down into our souls the gifts of the Holy Spirit.*

Lamb of God, Who takest away the sins of the world, *Grant us the Spirit of wisdom and piety.*

Come, Holy Spirit! Fill the hearts of Thy faithful, *And enkindle in them the fire of Thy love.*

Let Us Pray : Grant, O merciful Father, that Thy Divine Spirit may enlighten, inflame and purify us, that He may penetrate us with His heavenly dew and make us fruitful in good works, through Our Lord Jesus Christ, Thy Son, Who with Thee, in the unity of the same Spirit, liveth and reigneth forever and ever. Amen.

Other Prayers to the Holy Spirit

Come Holy Spirit, fill the hearts of your faithful and kindle in them the fire of your love. Send forth your Spirit and they shall be created. And You shall renew the face of the earth.

O, God, who by the light of the Holy Spirit, did instruct the hearts of the faithful, grant that by the same Holy Spirit we may be truly wise and ever enjoy His consolations, Through Christ Our Lord, Amen.

Mary Kloska

'Veni Creator'

Come, Holy Spirit, Creator blest,
and in our souls take up Thy rest;
come with Thy grace and heavenly aid
to fill the hearts which Thou hast made.

O comforter, to Thee we cry,
O heavenly gift of God Most High,
O fount of life and fire of love,
and sweet anointing from above.

Thou in Thy sevenfold gifts are known;
Thou, finger of God's hand we own;
Thou, promise of the Father, Thou
Who dost the tongue with power imbue.

Kindle our sense from above,
and make our hearts o'erflow with love;
with patience firm and virtue high
the weakness of our flesh supply.

Far from us drive the foe we dread,
and grant us Thy peace instead;
so shall we not, with Thee for guide,
turn from the path of life aside.

Oh, may Thy grace on us bestow
the Father and the Son to know;
and Thee, through endless times confessed,
of both the eternal Spirit blest.

Now to the Father and the Son,
Who rose from death, be glory given,
with Thou, O Holy Comforter,
henceforth by all in earth and heaven. Amen.

St. Augustine's Prayer to the Holy Spirit

Breathe into me, Holy Spirit, that my thoughts may all be holy. Move in me, Holy Spirit, that my work, too, may be holy. Attract my heart, Holy Spirit, that I may love only what is holy. Strengthen me, Holy Spirit, that I may defend all that is holy. Protect me, Holy Spirit, that I may always be holy.

St. Alphonsus Liguori's Prayer to the Holy Spirit

Holy Spirit, divine Consoler, I adore You as my true God, with God the Father and God the Son. I adore You and unite myself to the adoration You receive from the angels and saints.

I give You my heart and I offer my ardent thanksgiving for all the grace which You never cease to bestow on me.

O Giver of all supernatural gifts, who filled the soul of the Blessed Virgin Mary, Mother of God, with such immense favors, I beg You to visit me with Your grace and Your love and to grant me the gift of holy fear, so that it may act on me as a check to prevent me from falling back into my past sins, for which I beg pardon.

Grant me the gift of piety, so that I may serve You for the future with increased fervor, follow with more promptness Your holy inspirations, and observe your divine precepts with greater fidelity. Grant me the gift of knowledge, so that I may know the things of God and, enlightened by Your holy teaching, may walk, without deviation, in the path of eternal salvation.

Grant me the gift of fortitude, so that I may overcome courageously all the assaults of the devil, and all the dangers of this world which threaten the salvation of my soul.

Grant me the gift of counsel, so that I may choose what is more conducive to my spiritual advancement and may discover the wiles and snares of the tempter.

Grant me the gift of understanding, so that I may apprehend the divine mysteries and by contemplation of heavenly things detach my thoughts and affections from the vain things of this miserable world.

Grant me the gift of wisdom, so that I may rightly direct all my actions, referring them to God as my last end; so that, having loved Him and served Him in this life, I may have the happiness of possessing Him eternally in the next. Amen.

A Prayer to the Holy Spirit (by Cardinal Mercier)

O Holy Spirit, beloved of my soul, I adore You. Enlighten me, guide me, strengthen me, console me. Tell me what I should do; give me Your orders. I promise to submit myself to all that You desire of me and to accept all that You permit to happen to me. Let me only know Your Will.

Prayer for the Help of the Holy Spirit by St. Anthony of Padua

O God, send forth your Holy Spirit into my heart that I may perceive, into my mind that I may remember, and into my soul that I may meditate. Inspire me to speak with piety, holiness, tenderness and mercy. Teach, guide and direct my thoughts and senses from beginning to end. May your grace ever help and correct me, and may I be strengthened now with wisdom from on high, for the sake of your infinite mercy. Amen. -Saint Anthony of Padua

Litany for the Souls in Purgatory

O Jesus, Thou suffered and died that all mankind might be saved and brought to eternal happiness. Hear our pleas for further mercy on the souls of:

My dear parents and grandparents, My Jesus Mercy!
My brothers and sisters and other near relatives, My Jesus Mercy!
My godparents and sponsors of Confirmation, My Jesus Mercy!
My spiritual and temporal benefactors, My Jesus Mercy!
My friends and neighbors, My Jesus Mercy!
All for whom love or duty bids me pray, My Jesus Mercy!

Those who have suffered disadvantage or harm through me, My Jesus Mercy!
Those who have offended me, My Jesus Mercy!
Those whose release is near at hand, My Jesus Mercy!
Those who desire most to be united to Thee, My Jesus Mercy!
Those who endure the greatest sufferings, My Jesus Mercy! Those whose release is most remote, My Jesus Mercy!
Those who are least remembered, My Jesus Mercy!
Those who are most deserving on account of their services to the Church, My Jesus Mercy!

The rich, who are now the most destitute, My Jesus Mercy!
The mighty, who are now powerless, My Jesus Mercy!

The once spiritually blind, who now see their folly, My Jesus Mercy!

The frivolous, who spent their time in idleness, My Jesus Mercy!

The poor who did not seek the treasures of heaven, My Jesus Mercy!

The tepid who devoted little time to prayer, My Jesus Mercy!

The indolent who neglected to perform good works, My Jesus Mercy!

Those of little faith, who neglected the frequent reception of the Sacraments, My Jesus Mercy!

The habitual sinners, who owe their salvation to a miracle of grace, My Jesus Mercy!

Parents who failed to watch over their children, My Jesus Mercy!

Superiors who were not solicitous for the salvation of those entrusted to them, My Jesus Mercy!

Those who strove for worldly riches and pleasures, My Jesus Mercy!

The worldly minded, who failed to use their wealth and talent for the service of God, My Jesus Mercy!

Those who witnessed the death of others, but would not think of their own, My Jesus Mercy!

Those who did not provide for the life hereafter, My Jesus Mercy!

Those whose sentence is severe because of the great things entrusted to them, My Jesus Mercy!

The popes, kings, and rulers, My Jesus Mercy!

The bishops and their counselors, My Jesus Mercy!

My teachers and spiritual advisors, My Jesus Mercy!

The priests and religious of the Catholic Church, My Jesus Mercy!

The defenders of the Holy Faith, My Jesus Mercy!

Those who died on the battlefield, My Jesus Mercy!

Those who fought for their country, My Jesus Mercy!

Those who were buried in the sea, My Jesus Mercy!

Those who died of apoplexy, My Jesus Mercy!

Those who died of heart attacks, My Jesus Mercy!

Those who suffered and died of cancer, My Jesus Mercy!

Those who died suddenly in accidents, My Jesus Mercy!

Those who died without the last rites of the Church, My Jesus Mercy!

Those who shall die within the next twenty-four hours, My Jesus Mercy!

My own poor soul when I shall have to appear before Thy judgment seat, My Jesus Mercy!

PRAYER

Eternal rest grant unto them, O Lord, and let perpetual light shine upon them:

For evermore with Thy Saints, because Thou art gracious. May the prayer of Thy supplicant people, we beseech Thee, O Lord, benefit the souls of Thy departed servants and handmaids: that Thou mayest both deliver them from all their sins, and make them to be partakers of Thy redemption. Amen.

Eternal rest grant unto them, O Lord. And let perpetual light shine on them. Amen.

May their souls and the souls of all the faithful departed through the mercy of God, rest in peace. Amen

Chapter 5

Tuesday Prayers – to the Holy Angels

Consecration to the Holy Angels

O Holy Angels of God, here, in the presence of the Triune God and in the love of Jesus Christ, my Lord and Redeemer, I, N.N., poor sinner, want to make a covenant with you, who are his servants, so that in union with you, I might work with humility and fortitude for the glory of God and the coming of his Kingdom. Therefore, I implore you to assist me, especially – in the adoration of God and of the Most Holy Sacrament of the Altar, – in the contemplation of the word and the salvific works of God, -in the imitation of Christ and in the love of his Cross in a spirit of expiation, – in the faithful fulfillment of my mission within the Church, serving humbly after the example of Mary, my heavenly Mother, your Queen. And you, my good guardian angel, who continually behold the face of our Father in heaven, God entrusted me to you from the very beginning of my life. I thank you with all my heart for your loving care. I commit myself to you and promise you my love and fidelity. I beg you: protect me against my own weakness and against the attacks of the wicked spirits; enlighten my mind and my heart so that I may always know and accomplish the will of God; and lead me to union with God the Father, the Son, and the Holy Spirit. Amen.

The Congregation for the Doctrine of the Faith approved this Consecration prayer on May 31, 2000 for use in Opus Angelorum. © 2000 Congregazione dei Canonici Regolari della Santa Croce – Roma

Consecration to St. Michael the Archangel

Oh most noble Prince of the Angelic Hierarchies, valorous warrior of Almighty God and zealous lover of His glory, terror of the rebellious angels, and love and delight of all the just angels, my beloved Archangel Saint Michael, desiring to be numbered among your devoted servants, I, today offer and consecrate myself to you, and place myself, my family, and all I possess under your most powerful protection.

I entreat you not to look at how little, I, as your servant have to offer, being only a wretched sinner, but to gaze, rather, with favorable eye at the heartfelt affection with which this offering is made, and remember that if from this day onward I am under your patronage, you must during all my life assist me, and procure for me the pardon of my many grievous offenses, and sins, the grace to love with all my heart my God, my dear Savior Jesus, and my Sweet Mother Mary, and to obtain for me all the help necessary to arrive to my crown of glory.

Defend me always from my temporal and spiritual enemies, particularly in the last moments of my life. Come then, oh Glorious Prince, and succor me in my last struggle, and with your powerful weapon cast far from me into the infernal abysses that prevaricator and proud angel that one day you prostrated in the celestial battle. Amen.

Prayers From the Chaplet of St. Michael

1. By the intercession of St. Michael and the celestial Choir of Seraphim may the Lord make us worthy to burn with the fire of perfect charity. Amen.

2. By the intercession of St. Michael and the celestial Choir of Cherubim may the Lord grant us the grace to leave the ways of sin and run in the paths of Christian perfection. Amen. We pray for wisdom, knowledge, understanding, right judgment, counsel, truth and light.

3. By the intercession of St. Michael and the celestial Choir of Thrones may the Lord infuse into our hearts a true and sincere spirit of humility. Amen. We pray for Peace, purity, meekness, gentleness, humility, joy and docility.

4. By the intercession of St. Michael and the celestial Choir of Dominations may the Lord give us grace to govern our senses and overcome any unruly passions. Amen. We pray for God's will to be made known to us, for help in perplexities and for holy zeal, perseverance and confidence.

5. By the intercession of St. Michael and the celestial Choir of Virtues may the Lord preserve us from evil and falling into temptation. Amen. We pray for the grace to carry out the will of

God, for the government of seasons and elements, for those in public office and for extraordinary needs of mind and body.

6. By the intercession of St. Michael and the celestial Choir of Powers may the Lord protect our souls against the snares and temptations of the devil. Amen. We pray for the powers to fight against the evil spirits set to destroy the great plans of God. And we ask for strength, courage and fortitude.

7. By the intercession of St. Michael and the celestial Choir of Principalities may God fill our souls with a true spirit of obedience. Amen. We ask them to guard all nations and to help those in authority –those who govern bodies and souls.

8. By the intercession of St. Michael and the celestial Choir of Archangels may the Lord give us perseverance in faith and in all good works in order that we may attain the glory of Heaven. Amen.

9. By the intercession of St. Michael and the celestial Choir of Guardian Angels may the Lord grant us to be protected by them in this mortal life and conducted in the life to come to Heaven. Amen.

Concluding prayers:

O glorious prince St. Michael, chief and commander of the heavenly hosts, guardian of souls, vanquisher of rebel spirits, servant in the house of the Divine King and our admirable conductor, you who shine with excellence and superhuman virtue deliver us from all evil, who turn to you with confidence and enable us by your gracious protection to serve God more and more faithfully every day.

Pray for us, O glorious St. Michael, Prince of the Church of Jesus Christ, that we may be made worthy of His promises.

Almighty and Everlasting God, Who, by a prodigy of goodness and a merciful desire for the salvation of all men, has appointed the most glorious Archangel St. Michael Prince of Your Church, make us worthy, we ask You, to be delivered from all our enemies, that none of them may harass us at the hour of death, but that we may be conducted by him into Your Presence. This we ask through the merits of Jesus Christ Our Lord. Amen.

Litany to the Holy Angels

Lord have mercy. *Lord have mercy.*
Christ have mercy. *Christ have mercy.*
Lord have mercy. *Lord have mercy.*
Christ hear us. *Christ graciously hear us.*

God the Son, Redeemer of the world, *Have mercy on us.*

God the Holy Spirit, *Have mercy on us.*

Holy Trinity, One God, *Have mercy on us.*

Holy Mary, Queen of Angels, *pray for us.*

Holy Mother of God, *pray for us.*

Holy Virgins of virgins, *pray for us.*

Saint Michael, who was ever the defender of the people of God, *pray for us.*

St. Michael, who did drive from Heaven Lucifer and his rebel crew, *pray for us.*

St. Michael, who did cast down to Hell the accuser of our brethren, *pray for us.*

Saint Gabriel, who did expound to Daniel the Heavenly vision, *pray for us.*

St. Gabriel, who did foretell to Zachary the birth and ministry of John the Baptist, *pray for us.*

St. Gabriel, who did announce to the Blessed Mary the Incarnation of the Divine Word, *pray for us.*

St. Gabriel, who guided St. Joseph in dreams, *pray for us.*

Saint Raphael, who did lead Tobias safely through his journey to his home again, *pray for us.*

St. Raphael, who did deliver Sara from the devil and arranged her marriage, *pray for us.*

St. Raphael, who did restore sight to Tobias the elder, *pray for us.*

All ye holy Angels, who stand around the high and lofty throne of God, *pray for us.*

Who cry to Him continually: Holy, Holy, Holy, *pray for us.*

Who dispel the darkness of our minds and give us light, *pray for us.*

Who are the messengers of Heavenly things to men, *pray for us.*

Who have been appointed by God to be our Guardians, *pray for us.*

Who always behold the Face of our Father Who Is in Heaven, *pray for us.*

Who rejoice over one sinner doing penance, *pray for us.*

Who struck the Sodomites with blindness, *pray for us.*

Who led Lot out of the midst of the ungodly, *pray for us.*

Who ascended and descended on the ladder of Jacob, *pray for us.*

Who delivered the Divine Law to Moses on Mount Sinai, *pray for us.*

Who brought good tidings when Christ was born, *pray for us.*

Who ministered to Him in the desert, *pray for us.*

Who comforted Him in His agony, *pray for us.*

Who sat in white garments at His sepulcher, *pray for us.*

Who appeared to the disciples as He went up into Heaven, *pray for us.*

Who shall go before Him bearing the standard of the Cross when He comes to judge, *pray for us.*

Who shall gather together the elect at the End of the World, *pray for us.*

Who shall separate the wicked from among the just, *pray for us.*

Who offer to God the prayers of those who pray, *pray for us.*

Who assist us at the hour of death, *pray for us.*

Who carried Lazarus into Abraham's bosom, *pray for us.*

Who conduct to Heaven the Souls of the just, *pray for us.*

Who perform signs and wonders by the power of God, *pray for us.*

Who are sent to minister for those who shall receive the inheritance of salvation, *pray for us.*

Who are set over kingdoms and provinces, *pray for us.*

Who have often put to flight armies of enemies, *pray for us.*

Who have often delivered God's servants from prison and other perils of this life, *pray for us.*

Who have often consoled the holy Martyrs in their torments, *pray for us.*

Who cherish with particular care the Bishops of the Church, *pray for us.*

All ye holy orders of blessed spirits, *pray for us.*

From all dangers, *deliver us, O Lord.*

From the snares of the devil, *deliver us, O Lord.*

From all heresy and schism, *deliver us, O Lord.*

From plague, famine and war, *deliver us, O Lord.*

From sudden and unexpected death, *deliver us, O Lord.*

From everlasting death, *deliver us, O Lord.*

We sinners

    Beseech Thee to hear us.

Through the holy Angels, *we beseech Thee, hear us.*

That Thou wouldst spare us, *we beseech Thee, hear us.*

That Thou wouldst pardon us, *we beseech Thee, hear us.*

That Thou wouldst govern and preserve Thine Holy Church, *we beseech Thee, hear us.*

That Thou wouldst protect our bishop and all ministers of the

Church, *we beseech Thee, hear us.*

That Thou wouldst grant peace and security to all country rulers, *we beseech Thee, hear us.*

That Thou wouldst give and preserve the fruits of the earth, *we beseech Thee, hear us.*

That Thou wouldst grant eternal rest to all the Faithful departed, *we beseech Thee, hear us.*

Lamb of God, Who takes away the sins of the world, *Spare us, O Lord.*

Lamb of God, Who takes away the sins of the world, *Graciously hear us, O Lord.*

Lamb of God, Who takes away the sins of the world, *Have mercy on us.*

Bless the Lord, all ye Angels:

Thou who art mighty in strength, who fulfill His commandments, listening to the voice of His words.

He has given His Angels charge over you,
To keep you in all His ways.

Let Us Pray.

O God, Who doth arrange the services of Angels and men in a wonderful order, mercifully grant that our life may be protected on earth by those who always do Thy service in Heaven, through Jesus Christ Thy Son, Who with Thee and the Holy Spirit are one God, now and forever. Amen.

O God, Who in Thine unspeakable Providence sends Thy Angels to keep guard over us, grant us that we may be continually defended by their protection and may rejoice eternally in their company, through Jesus Christ Our Lord, Who livest and reignest with Thee, in the unity of the Holy Spirit, forever and ever. Amen.

Litany to St. Michael

Lord, have mercy on us. (Christ have mercy on us.) Lord, have mercy on us.

Christ, hear us. (*Christ graciously hear us.*)

God, the Father of heaven, (*have mercy on us.*)

God the Son, Redeemer of the world, (*have mercy on us.*)

God the Holy Ghost, (*have mercy on us.*)

Holy Trinity, one God, (*have mercy on us.*)

Holy Mary, Queen of Angels, *pray for us.*

St Michael, *pray for us.*

St Michael, filled with the wisdom of God,...

St Michael, perfect adorer of the Incarnate Word,

St Michael, crowned with honor and glory,

St Michael, most powerful Prince of the armies of the Lord,

St Michael, standard-bearer of the Most Holy Trinity,

St Michael, victor over Satan,

St Michael, guardian of Paradise,

St Michael, guide and comforter of the people of Israel,

St Michael, splendor and fortress of the Church Militant,

St Michael, honor and joy of the Church Triumphant,

St Michael, light of angels,

St Michael, bulwark of orthodox believers,

St Michael, strength of those who fight under the standard of the Cross,

St Michael, light and confidence of souls at the hour of death,

St Michael, our most sure aid,

St Michael, our help in all adversities,

St Michael, Herald of the Everlasting Sentence,

St Michael, Consoler of souls detained in the flames of Purgatory,

Thou whom the Lord has charged to receive souls after death,

St Michael, our Prince,

St Michael, our Advocate,

Lamb of God, who takest away the sins of the world, (*spare us, O Lord.*)

Lamb of God, who takest away the sins of the world, (*graciously hear us O Lord.*)

Lamb of God, who takest away the sins of the world, (*have mercy on us.*)

Christ hear us. (*Christ, graciously hear us.*)

Pray for us, O glorious St Michael, Prince of the Church of Jesus Christ. (*That we may be made worthy of His promises.*)

Let us pray:

Sanctify us, we beseech Thee, O Lord, with Thy holy blessing, and grant us, by the intercession of St.

Michael, that wisdom which teaches us to lay up treasures in Heaven by exchanging the goods of this world for those of eternity, Thou Who livest and reignest, world without end Amen.

Litany to St. Gabriel

Lord, have mercy on us. (Christ, have mercy on us.) Lord, have mercy on us.

Christ, hear us. (*Christ, graciously hear us.*)

God the Father of Heaven, *Have mercy on us.*

God the Son, Redeemer of the world, *Have mercy on us.*

God the Holy Spirit, *Have mercy on us.*

Holy Trinity, One God, *Have mercy on us.*

Holy Mary , Queen of Angels, *pray for us.*

Saint Gabriel, glorious Archangel, *pray for us.*

St. Gabriel, strength of God, *etc.*

St. Gabriel, who stands before the throne of God,

St. Gabriel, model of prayer,

St. Gabriel, herald of the Incarnation,

St. Gabriel, who revealed the glories of Mary,

St. Gabriel, Prince of Heaven,

St. Gabriel, ambassador of the Most High,

St. Gabriel, guardian of the Immaculate Virgin,

St. Gabriel, who foretold the greatness of Jesus,

St. Gabriel, peace and light of souls,

St. Gabriel, scourge of unbelievers,

St. Gabriel, admirable teacher,

St. Gabriel, strength of the just,

St. Gabriel, protector of the faithful,

St. Gabriel, first adorer of the Divine Word,

St. Gabriel, defender of the Faith,

St. Gabriel, zealous for the honor of Jesus Christ,

St. Gabriel, whom the Scriptures praise as the Angel sent by God to Mary, the Virgin,

St. Gabriel, who foretold the birth of St. John the Baptist,

St. Gabriel, who guided St. Joseph in Dreams,

Lamb of God, Who takest away the sins of the world, *Spare us, O Lord.*

Lamb of God, Who takest away the sins of the world, *Graciously hear us, O Lord.*

Lamb of God, Who takest away the sins of the world, *Have mercy on us.*

Christ, hear us.

Christ, graciously hear us.

V. Pray for us, blessed Archangel Gabriel,

R. *That we may be made worthy of the promises of Jesus Christ.*

Let Us Pray .

O blessed Archangel Gabriel, we beseech thee, intercede for us at the throne of Divine Mercy in our present necessities, that as thou didst announce to Mary the mystery of the Incarnation, so through thy prayers and patronage in Heaven we may obtain the benefits of the same, and sing the praise of God forever in the land of the living. R. Amen.

Litany to St. Raphael

Lord, have mercy on us. (*Christ have mercy on us.*) Lord, have mercy on us.

Christ hear us. (*Christ, graciously hear us.*)

God the Father of Heaven, *Have mercy on us.*

God the Son, Redeemer of the world, *Have mercy on us.*

God the Holy Spirit, *Have mercy on us.*

Holy Trinity, One God, *Have mercy on us.*

Holy Mary, Queen of Angels, *pray for us.*

St. Raphael, *pray for us.*

St. Raphael, filled with the mercy of God, *pray for us.*

St. Raphael, perfect adorer of the Divine Word, *pray for us.*

St. Raphael, terror of demons, *pray for us.*

St. Raphael, exterminator of vices, *pray for us.*

St. Raphael, health of the sick, *pray for us.*

St. Raphael, our refuge in all our trials, *pray for us.*

St. Raphael, guide of travelers, *pray for us.*

St. Raphael, consoler of prisoners, *pray for us.*

St. Raphael, joy of the sorrowful, *pray for us.*

St. Raphael, filled with zeal for the salvation of souls, *pray for us.*

St. Raphael, whose name means "God heals," *pray for us.*

St. Raphael, lover of chastity, *pray for us.*

St. Raphael, scourge of demons, *pray for us.*

St. Raphael, in pestilence, famine and war, *pray for us.*

St. Raphael, Angel of peace and prosperity, *pray for us.*

St. Raphael, endowed with the grace of healing, *pray for us.*

St. Raphael, sure guide in the paths of virtue and sanctification, *pray for us.*

St. Raphael, help of all those who implore thy assistance, *pray for us.*

St. Raphael, who was the guide and consolation of Tobias on his journey, *pray for us.*

St. Raphael, whom the Scriptures praise:

> "Raphael, the holy Angel of the Lord, was sent to cure," *pray for us.*

St. Raphael, our advocate, *pray for us.*

Lamb of God, Who takest away the sins of the world, *Spare us, O Lord.*

Lamb of God, Who takest away the sins of the world, *Graciously hear us, O Lord.*

Lamb of God, Who takes away the sins of the world, *Have mercy on us.*

Christ, hear us.

> *Christ, graciously hear us.*

Pray for us, St. Raphael, to the Lord Our God,

> *That we may be made worthy of the promises of Christ.*

Let Us Pray.

Lord, Jesus Christ, by the prayer of the Archangel Raphael, grant us the grace to avoid all sin and to persevere in every good work until we reach our Heavenly destination, Thou Who livest and reignest world without end. Amen.

Litany to the Guardian Angels

Lord, have mercy on us. (*Christ, have mercy on us.*) Lord, have mercy on us.

Jesus, hear us. *Jesus, graciously hear us.*

God the Father of Heaven, *Have mercy on us.*

God the Son, Redeemer of the world, *Have mercy on us.*

God the Holy Spirit, *Have mercy on us.*

Holy Trinity, One God, *Have mercy on us.*

Holy Mary, Queen of Angels, *pray for me.*

Angel of Heaven, who art my guardian, *pray for me.*

Angel of Heaven, whom I revere as my superior, *pray for me.*

Angel of Heaven, who dost give me charitable counsel, *pray for me.*

Angel of Heaven, who dost give me wise direction, *pray for me.*

Angel of Heaven, who dost take the place of a tutor, *pray for me.*

Angel of Heaven, who dost love me tenderly, *pray for me.*

Angel of Heaven, who art my consoler, *pray for me.*

Angel of Heaven, who art attached to me as a good brother, *pray for me.*

Angel of Heaven, who dost instruct me in the duties and truth of salvation, *pray for me.*

Angel of Heaven, who art to me a charitable shepherd, *pray for me.*

Angel of Heaven who art witness of all my actions, *pray for me.*

Angel of Heaven, who dost help me in all my undertakings, *pray for me.*

Angel of Heaven, who dost continually watch over me, *pray for me.*

Angel of Heaven, who dost intercede for me, *pray for me.*
Angel of Heaven, who dost carry me in thy hand, *pray for me.*
Angel of Heaven, who dost direct me in all my ways, *pray for me.*
Angel of Heaven, who dost defend me with zeal, *pray for me.*
Angel of heaven, who dost conduct me with wisdom, *pray for me.*
Angel of Heaven, who dost guard me from all danger, *pray for me.*
Angel of Heaven, who dost dissipate the darkness and enlighten
the mind, *pray for me.*

Lamb of God, Who takes away the sins of the world, *Spare us, O
Lord.*
Lamb of God, Who takes away the sins of the world, *Graciously
hear us, O Lord.*
Lamb of God, Who takes away the sins of the world, *Have mercy
on us, O Lord.*
Jesus, hear us. *Jesus, graciously hear us.*

Pray for us, O Guardian Angel,
That we may be made worthy of the promises of Christ.

Let Us Pray.

Almighty and eternal God, Who by an effect of Thine ineffable
bounty hast given to each of the faithful an angel to be the guardian
of body and soul, grant that I may have for him whom Thou hast
given me in Thy mercy so much respect and love, that, protected
by the gifts of Thy graces and by his help, I may merit to go to Thee

in Heaven, there to contemplate Thee with him and the other happy spirits in the brightness of Thy glory. Amen.

Chapter 6

Wednesday Prayers – to St. Joseph

Prayer/Consecration to St. Joseph's Holy Cloak

O Glorious Patriarch St Joseph, you who were chosen by God above all men to be the earthly head of the most holy of families, I beseech you to accept me within the folds of your Holy Cloak, that you may become the guardian and custodian of my body and soul.

From this moment on, I choose you as my father and brother, my protector and defender, my counsellor and guide, my patron and provider and I beseech you to place in your custody my body, mind, heart, soul, emotions, memory, past, present, future, my family and relationships, my home, possessions and finances, my work and ministry, my vocation, all that I am, all that I possess, my life and my death.

Look upon me as one of your children; defend me from the treachery of my enemies, both visible and invisible, assist me at all times in all my necessities; console me in the bitterness of my life, and especially at the hour of my death. Say but one word for me to the divine Redeemer whom you were deemed worthy to hold in your arms, and to the Blessed Virgin Mary, your most chaste spouse. Request for me those blessings which will lead me to salvation. Include me among those who are most dear to you and I shall set forth to prove myself worthy of your special patronage. Amen

Consecrations to St. Joseph

Act of Consecration to St. Joseph

O Glorious Patriarch and Patron of the Church! O Virgin Spouse of the Virgin Mother of God! O Guardian and Virginal Father of the Word Incarnate! In the presence of Jesus and Mary, I choose you this day to be my father, my guardian, my protector, my defender, my provider and my guide. O great St. Joseph, whom God has made the Head of the Holy Family, accept me, I beseech you, though utterly unworthy, to be a member of your "Holy House." Present me to your Immaculate Spouse; ask her also to adopt me as her child. With her, pray that I may constantly think of Jesus, and serve him faithfully to the end of my life. O Terror of Demons, increase in me virtue, protect me from the evil one, and help me not to offend God in any way.

O my Spiritual Father, I hereby consecrate myself to you. In faithful imitation of Jesus and Mary, I place myself and all my concerns under your care and protection. To you, after Jesus and Mary, I consecrate my body and soul, with all their faculties, my spiritual growth, my family and relationships, my home, my possessions, my finances, my work, my ministry, my vocation and all my affairs and undertakings. Forsake me not, but adopt me as a servant and child of the Holy Family. Watch over me at all times, but especially at the hour of my death. Console and strengthen me with the presence of Jesus and Mary so that, with you, I may praise and adore the Holy Trinity for all eternity. Amen

Act of Consecration to St. Joseph by St. Peter Julian Eymard

I consecrate myself to you, good St. Joseph, as my spiritual father. I choose you to rule my soul and to teach me the interior life, the life hidden away with Jesus, Mary, and yourself.

Above all, I want to imitate the humble silence with which you shrouded Jesus and Mary. For me everything lies in that self-abnegation like our Lord in his hidden life, making the world forget me by my silence and my practice of virtue.

I consecrate myself to you as my guide and model in all my duties so that I may learn to fulfill them with meekness and humility: with meekness toward my brothers and sisters, my neighbor, and all with whom I come in contact; with humility toward myself and simplicity before God.

I choose you, good saint, as my counselor, my confidant, my protector in all my difficulties and trials. I do not ask to be spared crosses and sufferings, but only from self-love which might take away their value by making me vain about them.

I choose you as my protector. Be my father as you were the father of the Holy Family at Nazareth. Be my guide; be my protector. I do not ask for temporal goods, greatness, or power. I ask only that I serve with fidelity and devotedness my divine King.

I shall honor, love, and serve you with Mary, my mother, and never shall I separate her name from yours.

O Jesus, give me Joseph for a father as you have given me Mary as a mother. Fill me with devotion, confidence, and filial love. Listen to my prayer. I know that you will. Already I feel more devout, more full of hope and confidence in good St. Joseph, your foster father and my spiritual father. Amen.

Act of Consecration to St. Joseph by St. Alphonsus Liguori

O Holy Patriarch, I rejoice with you at the exalted dignity by which you were deemed worthy to act as father to Jesus, to give him orders and to be obeyed by him whom heaven and earth obey. O great saint, as you were served by God, I too wish to be taken into your service. I choose you, after Mary, to be my chief advocate and protector. I promise to honor you every day by some special act of devotion and by placing myself under your daily protection. By that sweet company which Jesus and Mary gave you in your lifetime, protect me all through life, so that I may never separate myself from my God by losing his grace. My dear St. Joseph, pray to Jesus for me. Certainly, He can never refuse you anything, as He obeyed all your orders while on earth. Tell Him to detach me from all creatures and from myself, to inflame me with His holy love, and then to do with me what He pleases. By that assistance which Jesus and Mary gave you at death, I beg of you to protect me in a special way at the hour of my death, so that dying assisted by you, in the company of Jesus and Mary, I may go to thank you in paradise and, in your company, to praise my God for all eternity. Amen.

Act of Consecration to St. Joseph by St. Bernardine of Siena

Oh my beloved St. Joseph, adopt me as thy child. Take charge of my salvation; watch over me day and night; preserve me from the occasions of sin; obtain for me purity of body, mind, intention, heart, soul and spirit. Through thy intercession with Jesus, grant me a spirit of sacrifice, humility, self-denial, burning love for Jesus in the Blessed Sacrament, and a sweet and tender love for Mary, my mother. St. Joseph, be with me living, be with me dying, and obtain for me a favorable judgement from Jesus, my merciful Savior. Amen.

Litany of St. Joseph

Lord, have mercy. (*Christ, have mercy.*) Lord, have mercy.
Christ, hear us. (*Christ, graciously hear us.*)
God, the Father of Heaven, *have mercy on us.*
God the Son, Redeemer of the world, *have mercy on us.*
God the Holy Spirit, *have mercy on us.*
Holy Trinity, One God, *have mercy on us.*

Holy Mary, *pray for us (after each line)*

Saint Joseph, Renowned offspring of David,

Light of Patriarchs,

Spouse of the Mother of God,

Chaste guardian of the Virgin,

Foster-father of the Son of God,

Diligent protector of Christ,

Head of the Holy Family,

Joseph most just,

Joseph most merciful,

Joseph most chaste,

Joseph most prudent,

Joseph most strong,

Joseph most gentle,

Joseph most obedient,

Joseph most faithful,

Mirror of patience,

Lover of poverty,

Model of artisans,

Glory of home life,

Guardian of virgins,

Pillar of families,

Solace of the wretched,

Hope of the sick,

Patron of the dying,

Terror of demons,

Protector of Holy Church,

Lamb of God, who takes away the sins of the world, *Spare us, O Lord.*

Lamb of God, who takes away the sins of the world, *Graciously hear us, O Lord.*

Lamb of God, who takes away the sins of the world, *Have mercy on us.*

V. He made him the lord of His house:

R. *And ruler of all His substance.*

Let us pray.

O God, in Your loving providence chose Blessed St. Joseph to be the spouse of Your own most Holy Mother: grant us the favor to have him for our intercessor in heaven, whom we venerate as our defender on earth: You who live and reign, world without end. Amen.

33 Day Prayer to St. Joseph

Ever blessed and glorious Joseph, kind and loving father, and helpful friend of all in sorrow! You are the good father and protector of orphans, the defender of the defenseless, the patron of those in need and sorrow. Look kindly on my request. My sins have drawn down on me the just displeasure of my God, and so I am surrounded with unhappiness. To you, loving guardian of the Family of Nazareth, do I go for help and protection.

Listen, then, I beg you, with fatherly concern, to my earnest prayers, and obtain for me the favors I ask.

I ask it by the infinite mercy of the eternal Son of God, which moved Him to take our nature and to be born into this world of sorrow.

I ask it by the weariness and suffering you endured when you found no shelter at the inn of Bethlehem for the holy Virgin, nor a house where the Son of God could be born. Then, being everywhere refused, you had to allow the Queen of Heaven to give birth to the world's Redeemer in a cave.

I ask it by the loveliness and power of that sacred Name, Jesus, which you conferred on the adorable infant.

I ask it by that painful torture you felt at the prophecy of holy Simeon, which declared the Child Jesus and His holy Mother future victims of our sins and of their great love for us.

I ask it through your sorrow and pain of soul when the angel declared to you that the life of the Child Jesus was sought by His enemies. From their evil plan you had to flee with Him and His Blessed Mother to Egypt. I ask it by all the suffering, weariness, and labors of that long and dangerous journey.

I ask it by all your care to protect the Sacred Child and His Immaculate Mother during your second journey, when you were ordered to return to your own country. I ask it by your peaceful life in Nazareth where you met with so many joys and sorrows.

I ask it by your great distress when the adorable Child was lost to you and His Mother for three days. I ask it by your joy at finding Him in the Temple, and by the comfort you found at Nazareth, while living in the company of the Child Jesus. I ask it by the wonderful submission He showed in His obedience to you.

I ask it by the perfect love and conformity you showed in accepting the Divine order to depart from this life, and from the company of Jesus and Mary. I ask it by the joy which filled your soul, when the Redeemer of the world, triumphant over death and hell, entered into the possession of His kingdom and led you into it with special honors.

I ask it through Mary's glorious Assumption, and through that endless happiness you have with her in the presence of God.
O good father! I beg you, by all your sufferings, sorrows, and joys, to hear me and obtain for me what I ask.

(make your request)

Obtain for all those who have asked my prayers everything that is useful to them in the plan of God. Finally, my dear patron and father, be with me and all who are dear to me in our last moments, that we may eternally sing the praises of Jesus, Mary and Joseph.

Chapter 7

Thursday Prayers – for Priests and to the Blessed Sacrament

St. Therese of Lisieux's Prayer for Priests

O Jesus, I pray for your faithful and fervent priests;

for your unfaithful and tepid priests;

for your priests laboring at home or abroad in distant mission fields;

for your tempted priests;

for your lonely and desolate priests;

for your young priests;

for your dying priests;

for the souls of your priests in purgatory.

But above all, I recommend to you the priests dearest to me:

the priest who baptized me;

the priests who absolved me from my sins;

the priests at whose Masses I assisted and who gave me your Body and Blood in Holy Communion;

the priests who taught and instructed me; those who are in my family, those who I am friends with and those who the Lord has entrusted to my prayer in a special way;

all the priests to whom I am indebted in any other way, especially

_____.

O Jesus, keep them all close to your heart, and bless them abundantly in time and in eternity. Amen.

St. Theresa's Prayer for Priests

O Jesus, eternal Priest, keep your priests within the shelter of Your Sacred Heart, where none may touch them.

Keep unstained their anointed hands, which daily touch Your Sacred Body.

Keep unsullied their lips, daily purpled with your Precious Blood.

Keep pure and unearthly their hearts, sealed with the sublime mark of the priesthood.

Let Your holy love surround them and shield them from the world's contagion.

Bless their labors with abundant fruit and may the souls to whom they minister be their joy and consolation here and in heaven their beautiful and everlasting crown.

St.John Vianney's Prayer for Priests

God, please give to your Church today many more priests after your own heart.

May they be worthy representatives of Christ the Good Shepherd.

May they wholeheartedly devote themselves to prayer and penance; be examples of humility and poverty;

shining models of holiness;

tireless and powerful preachers of the Word of God;

zealous dispensers of your grace in the sacraments.

May their loving devotion to your Son Jesus in the Eucharist and to Mary his Mother be the twin fountains of fruitfulness for their ministry.

St. Pope John Paul II's Prayer for Priests to Our Blessed Mother

Mother of Jesus Christ and Mother of priests,
Accept this title which we bestow on you to celebrate your motherhood
and to contemplate with you the priesthood of your Son and of your sons,
O holy Mother of God.

Mother of Christ,
to the Messiah Priest you gave a body of flesh
through the anointing of the Holy Spirit
for the salvation of the poor and the contrite of heart;
guard priests in your heart and in the Church,
O Mother of the Savior.

Mother of Faith,
you accompanied to the Temple the Son of Man,
the fulfillment of the promises given to the fathers;
give to the Father for his glory the priests of your Son,
O Ark of the Covenant.

Mother of the Church,
with the disciples in the Upper Room

you prayed to the Spirit for the new People and their shepherds;

obtain for the Order of Presbyters a fullness of gifts,

O Queen of the Apostles.

Mother of Jesus Christ,

you were with Him at the beginning of His life and of His mission,

you sought the Master among the crowd,

you stood beside Him when he was lifted up from the earth

consumed as the one eternal sacrifice,

and you had John close by you, your son;

accept from the beginning those who have been called,

protect their growth, accompany your sons in their life and in their ministry,

O Mother of Priests.

St. Teresa of Calcutta's Prayer for Priests

Mary, Mother of Jesus, throw your mantle of purity over our priests.

Protect them, guide them, and keep them in your heart.

Be a Mother to them, especially in times of discouragement and loneliness.

Love them and keep them belonging completely to Jesus.

Like Jesus, they, too, are your sons, so keep their hearts pure and virginal.

Keep their minds filled with Jesus, and put Jesus always on their lips,
so that he is the one they offer to sinners and to all they meet.

Mary, Mother of Jesus, be their Mother,
loving them and bringing them joy.
Take special care of sick and dying priests, and the ones most tempted.
Remember how they spent their youth and old age,
their entire lives serving and giving all to Jesus.

Mary, bless them and keep a special place for them in your heart.
Give them a piece of your heart, so beautiful and pure and immaculate,
so full of love and humility, so that they, too, can grow in the likeness of Christ.
Dear Mary, make them humble like you, and holy like Jesus.

Fr. Benedict's Prayer for Priests

Lord Jesus Christ, eternal High Priest,
You offered yourself to the Father on the altar of the Cross
and through the outpouring of the Holy Spirit
gave Your priestly people a share in Your redeeming sacrifice.

Hear our prayer for the sanctification of our priests.
Grant that all who are ordained to the ministerial priesthood

may be ever more conformed to You, the Divine Master.

May they preach the Gospel with pure heart and clear conscience.

Let them be shepherds according to Your own Heart,

single-minded in service to You and to the Church

and shining examples of a holy, simple and joyful life.

Through the prayers of the Blessed Virgin Mary, Your Mother and ours,

draw all priests and the flocks entrusted to their care

to the fullness of eternal life where you live and reign

with the Father and the Holy Spirit, one God, forever and ever.

St. Faustina's Prayer for Priests

Heavenly Father, grant that our priests be strengthened and healed

by the power of the Eucharist they celebrate.

May the Word they proclaim give them courage and wisdom.

We pray that all those whom they seek to serve

May see in them the love and care of Jesus,

Our Eternal High Priest, who is Lord for ever and ever. Amen.

Mary, Mother of the Church, look tenderly upon your sons, our priests.

St Joseph, Patron of the Universal Church, pray for us all.

O my Jesus, I beg You on behalf of the whole Church:
Grant it love and the light of Your Spirit
and give power to the words of priests
so that hardened hearts might be brought to repentance
and return to You, O Lord.

Lord, give us holy priests;
You Yourself maintain them in holiness.
O Divine and Great High Priest,
may the power of Your mercy accompany them everywhere and
protect them
from the devil's snares which are continually being set for the souls
of priests.
May the power of Your mercy, O Lord,
shatter and bring to naught all that might tarnish the sanctity of
priests,
for You can do all things.

A Prayer for one Priest

O Jesus, Eternal High Priest, live in (name a priest),
act in him, speak in and through him.
Think Your thoughts in his mind,
love through his heart.
Give him Your Own dispositions and feelings.
Teach, lead and guide him always.
Correct, enlighten and expand his thoughts and behavior.

Enable him to give himself entirely to You.

Possess his soul;

take over his entire personality and life.

Replace him with Yourself.

Incline him to constant adoration and thanksgiving;

pray in and through him.

Let him live in You

and keep him in this intimate union always.

O Mary, Immaculate Conception,

Mother of Jesus and Mother of priests,

pray and intercede for *(name of priest)*. Amen.

Litany for Priests

Let us pray for the Holy Father: *fill him with courage and grace, Lord.*

Cardinals, archbishops, and bishops: *give them a shepherd's heart, Lord.*

Diocesan priests: *fill them with your Spirit, Lord.*

Priests in religious orders: *perfect them in their calling, Lord.*

Priests who are ill: *heal them, Lord.*

Priests who are in danger: *deliver them, Lord.*

Priests who are weak: *strengthen them, Lord.*

Priests who are poor: *relieve them, Lord.*

Priests who have lost their zeal: *renew them, Lord.*

Priests who are sad: *console them, Lord.*
Priests who are worried: *give them peace, Lord.*
Priests who are old: *sustain them, Lord.*
Priests who are alone: *accompany them, Lord.*

Missionary priests: *protect them, Lord.*
Priests who are preachers: *enlighten them, Lord.*
Priests who direct souls: *instruct them, Lord.*
Priests and religious who have died: *bring them to glory, Lord.*

For all priests: *give them Your wisdom and knowledge.*
For all priests: *give them Your understanding and counsel.*
For all priests: *give them reverence and awe of You.*
For all priests: *give them patience and love.*
For all priests: *give them obedience and kindness.*

For all priests: *give them a burning zeal for souls.*
For all priests: *give them virtues of faith, hope and love.*
For all priests: *give them an intense love for the Eucharist.*
For all priests: *give them loyalty to the teachings of the Church, the Holy Father and their Bishops.*

For all priests: *give them respect for life and human dignity.*
For all priests: *give them integrity, justice and mercy.*
For all priests: *give them humility, meekness and generosity.*

For all priests: *give them gentleness with souls and strength in their labors.*

For all priests: *give them peace in their sufferings.*

For all priests: *give them great love for the Trinity.*

For all priests: *give them great love for Mary, St Joseph, the angels and saints.*

For all priests: *let them be the light of Christ.*

For all priests: *let them be the salt of the earth.*

For all priests: *let them practice sacrifice and self-denial.*

For all priests: *let them be holy in body, mind, intention and spirit.*

For all priests: *let them be men of prayer.*

For all priests: *may faith shine forth in them.*

For all priests: *may they be concerned for our salvation.*

For all priests: *may they be faithful to their priestly vocation.*

For all priests: *may their hands know only how to bless and heal.*

For all priests: *may they burn with love for you.*

For all priests: *may all their steps be for the glory of God.*

For all priests: *may the Holy Spirit fill them, and give them His gifts in abundance.*

Let us pray.

Father, Son, and Holy Spirit,

hear the prayers we offer for our priests.

Let them know clearly the work that You are calling them to do.

Grant them every grace to answer Your call with courage, love, and lasting dedication to Your will.

We ask Mary's intercession as their loving mother. Amen.

Consecration to the Precious Blood of Priests and Those Destined to the Priesthood

1. My beloved Jesus, by the Precious Blood which Thou didst shed on the day of the Circumcision, deign to watch over the infancy and early education of the children whom Thou hast destined to minister at the altar, that they may be preserved spotless till consecrated to Thee by the holy unction. Bless the families that honor Thy Precious Blood, and spread this devotion by choosing from them a large number of vocations to the priesthood, and by maintaining their fervor till the close of their lives.

Our Lady of the Precious Blood, watch over the living chalices of the Blood of Jesus. Amen.

2. Lord Jesus, by the Precious Blood which Thou didst shed in the Garden of Olives, take pity on all aspirants to the priesthood who, through the temptations of the evil one or dread of the responsibilities of the sacred ministry, are in danger of losing their vocation. Impart to these tortured souls sufficient courage to make the sacrifices by which the Eucharistic Chalice must be purchased; and in return for their generosity, inebriate them deliciously at the

altar with the Blood which, in Heaven, will be their eternal source of delight.

Our Lady of the Precious Blood, watch over the living chalices of the Blood of Jesus. Amen.

3. Lord Jesus, by the Precious Blood shed in Thy painful Scourging, shield with Thy Own especial protection and that of Thine Immaculate Mother, all the ministers of the sanctuary, so that having renounced the goods of earth in order to belong entirely to Thee, they may every day offer and receive Thy Body and Blood with such pious dispositions as to enable Thee to find in their hearts "a paradise of delight."

Our Lady of the Precious Blood, watch over the living chalices of the Blood of Jesus. Amen.

4. Lord Jesus, by the Precious Blood which Thou didst shed in Thy Crowning with Thorns, we beseech Thee to maintain our clergy in such filial submission to the Holy See and its representatives, as will forever secure for them the veneration, confidence and docility of the faithful children of Holy Church.

Our Lady of the Precious Blood, watch over the living chalices of the Blood of Jesus. Amen.

5. Lord Jesus, by Thy Precious Blood shed on the way to Calvary, take pity on priests who are victims of injustice, and who, like their adorable Model, receive in return for their devotedness, but crosses, trials and persecutions.

Our Lady of the Precious Blood, watch over the living chalices of the Blood of Jesus. Amen.

6. Lord Jesus, by the Blood of Thy Crucifixion, inflame with ever-increasing zeal the dispensers of Thy Blood. Grant that thirsting like Thee for souls, they may continue the work of Thy Bloody Passion, increasing its efficacy by applying its merits. Succor, most of all, the poor missionaries, who after watering with their sweat and their tears the soil in which they have sown the divine seed, may still be called upon to dye with their blood the land upon which they planted the cross.

Our Lady of the Precious Blood, watch over the living chalices of the Blood of Jesus. Amen.

7. Lord Jesus, through the Blood and Water shed by Thee after death, take special pity, we beseech Thee, on those among Thy ministers who will soon be mown down by death. If, through human frailty, they have become the debtors of Your justice, grant that this very day, the infinitely Precious Blood may discharge their obligations.

Our Lady of the Precious Blood, watch over the living chalices of the Blood of Jesus. Amen.

Prayer for Priests

Keep them, I pray Thee, dearest Lord, keep them, for they are Thine
– Thy priests whose lives burn out before Thy consecrated shrine.

Keep them, for they are in the world, though from the world apart;
when earthly pleasures tempt, allure – shelter them in Thy heart.

Keep them, and comfort them in hours of loneliness and pain,
when all their lives of sacrifice for souls seems but in vain.

Keep them, and O remember, Lord, they have no one but Thee,
yet they have only human hearts, with human frailty.

Keep them as spotless as the Host, that daily they caress;
their every thought and word and deed, Deign, dearest Lord, to bless.

St. Vincent Pallotti's Prayer to the Blessed Sacrament

Jesus in the Eucharist, Our God and our King –pray for us!
Jesus in the Eucharist, Our Creator and Redeemer –pray for us!

Jesus in the Eucharist, Our Physician and our Medicine –pray for us!

Jesus in the Eucharist, Our Food and our Grace –pray for us!

Jesus in the Eucharist, Our Greatest Good and Happiness –pray for us!

Jesus in the Eucharist, Infinitely loving and worthy of love –pray for us!

Jesus in the Eucharist, You are the greatest and most holy of our mysteries –pray for us!

Litany of the Most Blessed Sacrament

(*Written by St. Peter Julian Eymard, the founder of the Blessed Sacrament Fathers.*)

Lord, have mercy. R. *Lord, have mercy.*

Christ, have mercy. R. *Christ, have mercy.*

Lord, have mercy. R. *Lord, have mercy.*

Christ, hear us. R. *Christ, graciously hear us.*

God the Father of Heaven, R. *have mercy on us.*

God the Son, Redeemer of the world, R. *have mercy on us.*

God the Holy Spirit, R. *have mercy on us.*

Holy Trinity, one God, R. *have mercy on us.*

Jesus, Eternal High Priest of the Eucharistic Sacrifice, R. *have mercy on us.*

Jesus, Divine Victim on the Altar for our salvation, R. *have mercy on us.*

Jesus, hidden under the appearance of bread, R. *have mercy on us.*

Jesus, dwelling in the tabernacles of the world, R. *have mercy on us.*

Jesus, really, truly and substantially present in the Blessed Sacrament, R. *have mercy on us.*

Jesus, abiding in Your fullness, Body, Blood, Soul and Divinity, R. *have mercy on us.*

Jesus, Bread of Life, R. *have mercy on us.*

Jesus, Bread of Angels, R. *have mercy on us.*

Jesus, with us always until the end of the world, R. *have mercy on us.*

Sacred Host, summit and source of all worship and Christian life, R. *have mercy on us.*

Sacred Host, sign and cause of the unity of the Church, R. *have mercy on us.*

Sacred Host, adored by countless angels, R. *have mercy on us.*

Sacred Host, spiritual food, R. *have mercy on us.*

Sacred Host, Sacrament of love, R. *have mercy on us.*

Sacred Host, bond of charity, R. *have mercy on us.*

Sacred Host, greatest aid to holiness, R. *have mercy on us.*

Sacred Host, gift and glory of the priesthood, R. *have mercy on us.*

Sacred Host, in which we partake of Christ, R. *have mercy on us.*

Sacred Host, in which the soul is filled with grace, R. *have mercy on us.*

Sacred Host, in which we are given a pledge of future glory, R. *have mercy on us.*

Blessed be Jesus in the Most Holy Sacrament of the Altar.

Blessed be Jesus in the Most Holy Sacrament of the Altar.

Blessed be Jesus in the Most Holy Sacrament of the Altar.

For those who do not believe in Your Eucharistic presence, R. *have mercy, O Lord.*

For those who are indifferent to the Sacrament of Your love, R. *have mercy on us.*

For those who have offended You in the Holy Sacrament of the Altar, R. *have mercy on us.*

That we may show fitting reverence when entering Your holy temple, R. *we beseech You, hear us.*

That we may make suitable preparation before approaching the Altar, R. *we beseech You, hear us.*

That we may receive You frequently in Holy Communion with real devotion and true humility, R. *we beseech You, hear us.*

That we may never neglect to thank You for so wonderful a blessing, R. *we beseech You, hear us.*

That we may cherish time spent in silent prayer before You, R. *we beseech You, hear us.*

That we may grow in knowledge of this Sacrament of

sacraments, R. *we beseech You, hear us.*

That all priests may have a profound love of the Holy Eucharist, R. *we beseech You, hear us.*

That they may celebrate the Holy Sacrifice of the Mass in accordance with its sublime dignity, R. *we beseech You, hear us.*

That we may be comforted and sanctified with Holy Viaticum at the hour of our death, R. *we beseech You, hear us.*

That we may see You one day face to face in Heaven, R. *we beseech You, hear us.*

Lamb of God, You take away the sins of the world, R. *spare us, O Lord.*

Lamb of God, You take away the sins of the world, R. *graciously hear us, O Lord.*

Lamb of God, You take away the sins of the world, R. *have mercy on us, O Lord.*

V. O Sacrament Most Holy, O Sacrament Divine,
R. *all praise and all thanksgiving be every moment Thine.*

Let us pray,
Most merciful Father, You continue to draw us to Yourself through the Eucharistic Mystery.

Grant us fervent faith in this Sacrament of love, in which Christ the Lord Himself is contained, offered and received. We make this prayer through the same Christ our Lord. R. Amen.

Padre Pio's Prayer After Communion

Stay with me, Lord, for without Thy Presence I forget Thee;
Thou knowest how easily I abandon Thee.
Stay with me, Lord, for without Thy Strength I fall;
Thou knowest how weak I am.
Stay with me Lord, for without Thee my fervor fails;
Thou art my life.
Stay with me Lord, for without Thee I am in darkness;
Thou art my light.
Stay with me Lord and show me Thy Will,
Stay with me Lord and let me hear Thy Voice,
Stay with me Lord that I may follow Thee,
Stay with me Lord that I may love Thee more,
Stay with me Lord that I may stay with Thee.
If Thou would'st have me to be faithful, stay with me Lord.

Stay with me Jesus, for though my soul is poor, it desires to be an abode of love for Thee, a place of consolation.
Stay with me Jesus, for it is getting late; the day is ending, life is passing; death, judgement, eternity are coming soon. Now I must muster all my forces so that I do not faint on the road. I have great need for Thee on this journey. It is getting late and death is approaching –Darkness, temptations, dryness, crosses and troubles beset me –and, oh, how much I need Thee, my good Jesus, in this night of exile.

Stay with me Jesus because this night of life is so full of dangers and I have such need of Thee.

Grant that, like Thy disciples, I may recognize Thee in the breaking of the bread.

Grant that the Eucharistic union may be the light which casts out the darkness, the force to sustain me and the one means to sanctify my soul.

Stay with me Lord because, when death arrives, if I cannot be really with Thee in Holy Communion, then I shall wish to remain united with Thee at least through Grace and Love.

Stay with me Jesus. I do not ask Thee for divine consolation because I deserve it but I beg of Thee with all my strength for the gift of Thy most Holy Presence.

Stay with me Lord –Thee alone I seek; Thy Love, Thy Grace, Thy Will, Thy Heart, Thy Spirit –for I love Thee. Thee alone I love; Let me seek no other reward but the increase of that love, that my love may be real and firm and practical. I ask no more than to love Thee with all my heart on earth and to follow Thee with all-perfected love for all eternity. Amen.

Chapter 8

Friday's Prayers –To Jesus' Passion, Sacred Heart and Precious Blood

Consecration to the Sacred Heart

<u>Act of Consecration to the Sacred Heart of Jesus:</u>

Most Sacred Heart of Jesus, Abyss of Mercy and Source of every grace and blessing, I consecrate and unite myself to You without exception or reserve – all that I am and all that I have, both temporal and spiritual, past, present, and future, through the Immaculate Heart of Mary, your Mother. I leave myself entirely at Your disposal with complete confidence in Your Mercy and Love, and beg You to look upon my offering and use me for Your own glory, for the honor of Your Mother, and for the salvation of souls. Help me to seek You alone in all things. Hide me in the shelter of Your Most Sacred Heart and be my only consolation and refuge.

Grant me the graces I need to joyfully accept the Cross daily, to lead a holy life, and to die a holy death in Your service. Help me to trust completely in Your Mercy and Love and never to fear to humbly throw myself before the infinite ocean of mercy which is Your Most Sacred Heart. Through this weak and miserable instrument that I am, may Your Mercy, Love, glory and power shine forth. Above all, set my heart on fire with the Flame of Love which burns in Your Most Sacred Heart, and teach me how to return love for Your Love. Most Sacred Heart of Jesus, have mercy on me. I put all my trust in You.

Consecration of One's Family to the Sacred Heart

Prostrate before You, Lord Jesus Christ, we consecrate to Your Sacred Heart ourselves and everything dear to us: our thoughts, words and actions; our sorrows, our hopes, our relatives and friends. We desire to belong entirely to You, to know all things, and to despise the pleasures, riches and honors of this world and everything which could be an obstacle in Your service.

Sacred Heart of Jesus, teach us, by Your example in the stable of Bethlehem and by Your whole life, meekness and humility. Teach us, by Your agony and sufferings on the Cross, patience and resignation to the holy Will of God. Teach us, in the mystery of the holy Eucharist, to admire Your power, wisdom and love. Three hundred years ago, You revealed to Saint Margaret Mary Your desire to receive the special homage of Your creatures. In obedience to that divine entreaty, behold us at Your feet to consecrate to Your service and love our hearts, our family and our home in a special manner.

Heart of Jesus, in the name of Mary and under the patronage of Saint Joseph we consecrate to You our whole household. Like Nazareth, may it always be a center of faith, hope, charity and peace; a hive of prayer and true zeal for Your glory. Guide our lives, direct our steps, and sustain us in all our ways. We earnestly consecrate to You all the trials, afflictions, joys and events of our domestic life.

We beseech You to pour Your blessing upon every member of this family: those who are gathered here and those who are absent; those who are living and those who are dead. With confidence, we entrust them all to You. If, among them, there be any who have lost Your grace and grieved Your loving Heart by sin, with deepest sorrow we now desire to offer reparation and implore forgiveness for them.

We beg Your mercy and grace, also, for every family in the whole world. O Sacred Heart, shelter the cradle of the newborn babe; bless the child at school; guide the vocation of young men and women; sweeten the lot of the sufferer; support the aged; console the widow; be a Father to the orphan.

O Sacred Heart of Jesus, we entrust to You our own dear country and all those, who govern us.

O Jesus, source and infinite ocean of mercy, we beseech You assist us in the sufferings and agony of death. Unite us, then, still more closely to Your Heart and to the Heart of Your Immaculate Mother. Be our refuge and our place of rest; and when our souls have taken their flight to dwell forever in Your Sacred Heart, may we see again in heaven every member of this family which we now so earnestly and unitedly desire to consecrate without reserve to You. Amen.

Private Act of Consecration to the Sacred Heart written by St. Margaret Mary Alacoque:

O Sacred Heart of Jesus, to Thee I consecrate and offer up my person and my life, my actions, trials, and sufferings, that my entire being may henceforth only be employed in loving, honoring and glorifying Thee. This is my irrevocable will, to belong entirely to Thee, and to do all for Thy love, renouncing with my whole heart all that can displease Thee.

I take Thee, O Sacred Heart, for the sole object of my love, the protection of my life, the pledge of my salvation, the remedy of my frailty and inconstancy, the reparation for all the defects of my life, and my secure refuge at the hour of my death. Be Thou, O Most Merciful Heart, my justification before God Thy Father, and screen me from His anger which I have so justly merited. I fear all from my own weakness and malice, but placing my entire confidence in Thee, O Heart of Love, I hope all from Thine infinite Goodness. Annihilate in me all that can displease or resist Thee. Imprint Thy pure love so deeply in my heart that I may never forget Thee or be separated from Thee.

I beseech Thee, through Thine infinite Goodness, grant that my name be engraved upon Thy Heart, for in this I place all my happiness and all my glory, to live and to die as one of Thy devoted servants. Amen.

Consecration to the Sacred Heart by Blessed Mary of the Divine Heart

My most loving Jesus, I consecrate myself today anew and without reserve to Your divine Heart. I consecrate to You my body with all its senses, my soul with all its faculties: my whole being. I consecrate to You all my thoughts, words and actions; all my sufferings and labors; all my hopes, consolations and joys; and, above all, I consecrate to You my poor heart, that it may love only You and be consumed as a victim in the fire of Your love. Accept, O Jesus, my most loving spouse, the desire that I have to console Your divine Heart and to be Yours forever. Possess me in such a manner that henceforward I may have no other liberty than that of loving You, no other life than that of suffering and dying for You.

I place in You unlimited trust and I hope, from Your infinite mercy, for the pardon of my sins. I place in Your hands all my cares, especially that of my eternal salvation. I promise to love and honor You to the last moment of my life, and to propagate, with the help of Your divine grace and as far as I am able, devotion to Your Sacred Heart. Dispose of me, O divine Heart of Jesus, according to Your pleasure; I desire no other recompense than Your greater glory and Your holy love.

Grant me the grace to find my dwelling place in Your Sacred Heart where I desire to pass every day of my life and where I wish to breathe my last breath. Make my heart Your abode, the place of Your repose, so that we may remain intimately united until, finally,

I may praise, love, and possess You for all eternity, singing forever the infinite mercy of Your Sacred Heart. Amen.

Long Form of Consecration of Oneself and Enthronement of One's Home to the Sacred Heart

O most amiable and adorable Heart of Jesus, O Heart infinitely compassionate and merciful, my refuge in all dangers, my hope in all trials, my comfort and consolation in all sorrows, behold me humbly prostrate before You to implore Your mercy, to claim Your protection, and to offer myself entirely to You. You see the dangers that surround me, the storms by which I am assailed. The powers of darkness have risen against Your holy Church and against me, Your unworthy but devoted servant. They have laid waste Your inheritance, they have overturned Your altars, they have persecuted those that love and honor Your sacred Name. And now they glory in the evil which they have done and daily boast that they have triumphed over You and Your Church, and have destroyed Your worship from the face of the earth. But You are almighty, and who shall resist You? You will arise in Your power and Your enemies shall perish from before Your face. You will command the winds and the waves and there shall be a great calm. Animated with this confidence in Your power and Your love, O divine Heart, I present my supplication on this day of my solemn Consecration to You. Deign to receive my offering, unworthy as it is, and grant my prayer for the Church and for Your devoted Marian Catechists who solemnly dedicate themselves to Your honor. O merciful Heart, ever open to admit me into Your sacred and secure asylum. I, *(state your name),* Your servant, desiring to give You a proof of my devotion and to receive from You the assistance and protection which I need in these calamitous times for the Church, for the Holy See, and for myself, do on this day publicly and solemnly consecrate myself entirely to You; my life and labors; my thoughts, words, actions, and sufferings. I pledge myself to You as Your devoted servant forever. I consecrate to You my person, my home, my occupation, my ministry, my vocation and my family, and all those for whose spiritual good I labor in Your service, that Your Spirit may reign over them, Your love sustain them, Your grace sanctify them and make them at all times pleasing to Your sight.

O sweet and adorable Heart of Jesus, accept this holocaust which I offer; inflame it with Your divine love, that it may ascend before You in an odor of sweetness; and that, united with Your infinite merits, it may bring down upon me, upon Your holy Church, upon our Holy Father, our much afflicted Pontiff, His Holiness Pope _____, and upon all members of our organization the abundance of Your blessing, the heavenly showers of Your graces, the rich treasures which You have promised to those who would honor You. I make my Consecration, uniting my heart to the Immaculate Heart of Mary and begging the Virgin Mother of God to present it to You. Through her maternal intercession may I do always what You, her Son, tell me to do for Your glory and for the salvation of souls. Throw around me, Your servant, the shield of Your protection, guard me against the malice of the wicked, who hate Your Church because it is Yours and persecute me because I love Your holy Name and defend Your honor. Let me find in You my refuge, my consolation, my hope. Be You my support in life, my confidence in death, my eternal enjoyment in Heaven.

By this consecration and enthronement of the Sacred Heart, we link the tabernacle of our parish church to our home, inviting Our Lord to be our constant and most intimate companion.

Holy Mary, Virgin Mother of God, who was conceived without original sin, we choose you this day as the Lady and Mistress of this house, we beseech you, through your Immaculate Conception, to preserve it from pestilence, fire, and water, from lightening and tempests; from robbery and vandalism, from schism and heresy; from earthquake, war, sudden death, violence, abuse, division, discouragement, unfaithfulness, all sin and all evil.

Bless and protect, O Holy Virgin, all of those who dwell herein; obtain for us the grace to avoid all sin, fill each of us with the grace to love as your Son Jesus loved, and save us from every misfortune and accident.

Through the power of Our Lord Jesus Christ, I consecrate this home and property to the Sacred Heart of Jesus and the Immaculate Heart of Mary. In the Name of Jesus Christ and through the power of His Blood I command you satan to leave this ground, home and my life, family, work, ministry and relationships that all may be holy. I call upon the Holy Spirit to fill my life, my family and relationships, work and ministry, this home and property and I bless all of this in the name of the Father and of the Son and of the Holy Spirit, Amen.

Litany to the Sacred Heart

Lord, have mercy on us.
Christ, have mercy on us.
Lord, have mercy on us.
Christ, hear us.
Christ, graciously hear us.
God the Father of Heaven, *have mercy on us.*
(Repeat *have mercy on us.* after each line)
God the Son, Redeemer of the world,
God the Holy Spirit,
Holy Trinity, one God,
Heart of Jesus, Son of the Eternal Father,
Heart of Jesus, formed by the Holy Spirit in the Virgin Mother's womb,
Heart of Jesus, substantially united to the Word of God,
Heart of Jesus, of infinite majesty,
Heart of Jesus, holy temple of God,
Heart of Jesus, tabernacle of the Most High,
Heart of Jesus, house of God and gate of heaven,
Heart of Jesus, glowing furnace of charity,

Heart of Jesus, vessel of justice and love,

Heart of Jesus, full of goodness and love,

Heart of Jesus, abyss of all virtues,

Heart of Jesus, most worthy of all praise,

Heart of Jesus, King and center of all hearts,

Heart of Jesus, in whom are all the treasures of wisdom and knowledge,

Heart of Jesus, in whom dwells all the fullness of the Godhead,

Heart of Jesus, in whom the Father was well pleased,

Heart of Jesus, of whose fullness we have all received,

Heart of Jesus, desire of the everlasting hills,

Heart of Jesus, patient and rich in mercy,

Heart of Jesus, rich to all who call upon You,

Heart of Jesus, fount of life and holiness,

Heart of Jesus, propitiation for our offenses,

Heart of Jesus, overwhelmed with reproaches,

Heart of Jesus, bruised for our iniquities,

Heart of Jesus, obedient even unto death,

Heart of Jesus, pierced with a lance,

Heart of Jesus, source of all consolation,

Heart of Jesus, our life and resurrection,

Heart of Jesus, our peace and reconciliation,

Heart of Jesus, victim for our sins,

Heart of Jesus, salvation of those who hope in You,

Heart of Jesus, hope of those who die in You,

Heart of Jesus, delight of all saints,

Lamb of God, who takest away the sins of the world, *Spare us, O Lord.*

Lamb of God, who takest away the sins of the world, *Graciously hear us, O Lord.*

Lamb of God, who takest away the sins of the world, *Have mercy on us.*

Jesus, meek and humble of Heart, *Make our hearts like unto Thine. Let us pray.*

Almighty and eternal God, look upon the Heart of Thy most beloved Son and upon the praises and satisfaction which He offers Thee in the name of sinners; and to those who implore Thy mercy, in Thy great goodness, grant forgiveness in the name of the same Jesus Christ, Thy Son, who livest and reignest with Thee forever and ever. Amen.

Consecration to the Precious Blood

O Jesus, fairest of the children of men, Thou Whom I see crushed beneath the weight of my sins, covered with wounds, Thy hands and feet pierced with nails, Thy side opened with a lance, I adore Thee and recognize Thee as my Lord and my God and as my beloved Redeemer. Pierced with grief at sight of the Blood flowing from Thy wounds for the redemption of souls, I feel irresistibly urged to consecrate myself to the worship of this regenerating Blood and, by an exemplary life, to atone for all the profanations of this Divine Blood and for those which It still receives daily in the veins of Thy Sacred Body present mystically on the altar. By this consecration --- which I beg Thee to accept, O my Savior, I desire to spend my whole life in proving to Thee my gratitude and my love by paying frequent homage to Thy Precious Blood and by propagating this devotion as far as is in my power. I desire every pulsation of my heart to be a renewal of this consecration, a constantly repeated act of love for this redeeming Blood, a perpetual offering of Its merits in behalf of sinners and all the souls dear to me, and a hymn of unceasing praise in union with that of the Saints and all the blessed in Heaven: *"To the Lamb Who redeemed us in His Blood, be honor and glory and benediction forever."*

O Mary, mother of the Divine Redeemer, obtain for me the grace of adoring fervently throughout my life the Blood of thy Divine Son and of singing forever Its mercies in Heaven. Amen.

Litany to the Precious Blood

Lord, have mercy.   *Lord, have mercy.*

Christ, have mercy.   *Christ, have mercy on us.*

Lord, have mercy.   *Lord, have mercy.*

Jesus, hear us.   *Jesus, graciously hear us.*

God, the Father of Heaven, *Have mercy on us.*

God, the Son, Redeemer of the world, *Have mercy on us.*

God, the Holy Spirit, *Have mercy on us.*

Holy Trinity, One God, *Have mercy on us.*

Blood of Christ, only-begotten Son of the Eternal Father, *Save us.*

Blood of Christ, Incarnate Word of God, *Save us.*

Blood of Christ, of the New and Eternal Testament, *Save us.*

Blood of Christ, falling upon the earth in the Agony, *Save us.*

Blood of Christ, shed profusely in the Scourging, *Save us.*

Blood of Christ, flowing forth in the Crowning with Thorns, *Save us.*

Blood of Christ, poured out on the Cross, *Save us.*

Blood of Christ, price of our salvation, *Save us.*

Blood of Christ, without which there is no forgiveness. *Save us.*

Blood of Christ, Eucharistic drink and refreshment of souls, *Save us.*

Blood of Christ, stream of mercy, *Save us.*

Blood of Christ, victor over demons, *Save us.*

Blood of Christ, courage of Martyrs, *Save us.*

Blood of Christ, strength of Confessors, *Save us.*

Blood of Christ, bringing forth Virgins, *Save us.*

Blood of Christ, help of those in peril, *Save us.*

Blood of Christ, relief of the burdened, *Save us.*

Blood of Christ, solace in sorrow, *Save us.*

Blood of Christ, hope of the penitent, *Save us.*

Blood of Christ, consolation of the dying, *Save us.*

Blood of Christ, peace and tenderness of hearts, *Save us.*

Blood of Christ, pledge of eternal life, *Save us.*

Blood of Christ, freeing souls from purgatory, *Save us.*

Blood of Christ, most worthy of all glory and honor, *Save us.*

Lamb of God, who takes away the sins of the world, *Spare us, O Lord.*

Lamb of God, who takes away the sins of the world, *Graciously hear us, O Lord.*

Lamb of God, who takes away the sins of the world, *Have mercy on us, O Lord.*

You have redeemed us, O Lord, in your Blood.

And made us, for our God, a kingdom.

Let us pray:

Almighty and eternal God, you have appointed your only-begotten Son the Redeemer of the world, and willed to be appeased by his Blood. Grant we beg of you, that we may worthily adore this price of our salvation, and through its power be safeguarded from the evils of the present life, so that we may rejoice in its fruits forever in heaven. Through the same Christ our Lord. Amen.

Act of Consecration to the Precious Blood and the Blessed Virgin for Children

Blood of my Savior, a thousand times adorable! Blood a thousand times Precious! Thou, Which dost adorn the Baptismal innocence of children, deign to bless this young soul whom we consecrate to Thee this day. O sweet Jesus! hide beneath the vivifying waves of Thy Most Precious Blood thy little *[name]* so that he [she] may grow in grace and holiness all the days of his [her] life. Deign to look upon him [her] as a perpetual adorer of Thy Divine Blood in as far as the designs of Providence will permit and grant that all his [her] prayers, deeds and sacrifices may be so many acts of reparation and love.

O Immaculate Virgin, ever spotless through the Blood of Jesus, thou who art called the "Flower of the Field" and the "Lily of the Valley," look down lovingly from thy Heavenly throne upon this dear child; may he [she] grow up also under thy maternal care, shielded by thy blessings, and may every day of his [her] life be marked by thy benefits.

Most Holy Virgin whom the Church calls "Morning Star," shine upon this soul now commencing his [her] earthly pilgrimage, preserve him [her] from all harm, and until the last moment of his [her] life, may he [she] keep pure and unsullied the robe with which, through the Blood of Jesus, he [she] was robed in holy Baptism. Take his [her] family also under thy protection, O Mary. Bless his [her] pious parents, remove far from them every temporal or spiritual misfortune, and may peace, charity and all virtues dear to thy pure and holy heart dwell ever in their midst. Amen.

Chapter 9

Saturday Prayers – To Our Lady

Consecration to Our Lady by St. Louis de Montfort

O Eternal and incarnate Wisdom! O sweetest and most adorable Jesus! True God and true man, only Son of the Eternal Father, and of Mary, always virgin! I adore Thee profoundly in the bosom and splendors of Thy Father during eternity; and I adore Thee also in the virginal bosom of Mary, Thy most worthy Mother, in the time of Thine incarnation.

I give Thee thanks for that Thou hast annihilated Thyself, taking the form of a slave in order to rescue me from the cruel slavery of the devil. I praise and glorify Thee for that Thou hast been pleased to submit Thyself to Mary, Thy holy Mother, in all things, in order to make me Thy faithful slave through her.

But, alas! Ungrateful and faithless as I have been, I have not kept the promises which I made so solemnly to Thee in my Baptism; I have not fulfilled my obligations; I do not deserve to be called Thy child, nor yet Thy slave; and as there is nothing in me which does not merit Thine anger and Thy repulse, I dare not come by myself before Thy most holy and august Majesty. It is on this account that I have recourse to the intercession of Thy most holy Mother, whom Thou hast given me for a mediatrix with Thee. It is through her that I hope to obtain of Thee contrition, the pardon of my sins, and the acquisition and preservation of wisdom.

Hail, then, O Immaculate Mary, living tabernacle of the Divinity, where the Eternal Wisdom willed to be hidden and to be adored by angels and by men! Hail, O Queen of Heaven and earth, to whose empire everything is subject which is under God. Hail, O sure refuge of sinners, whose mercy fails no one. Hear the desires which I have of the Divine Wisdom; and for that end receive the vows and offerings which in my lowliness I present to thee.

I, N_____, a faithless sinner, renew and ratify today in thy hands the vows of my Baptism; I renounce forever Satan, his pomps and works; and I give myself entirely to Jesus Christ, the Incarnate Wisdom, to carry my cross after Him all the days of my life, and to be more faithful to Him than I have ever been before. In the presence of all the heavenly court I choose thee this day for my Mother and Mistress. I deliver and consecrate to thee, as thy slave, my body and soul, my goods, both interior and exterior, and even the value of all my good actions, past, present and future; leaving to thee the entire and full right of disposing of me, and all that belongs to me, without exception, according to thy good pleasure, for the greater glory of God in time and in eternity.

Receive, O benignant Virgin, this little offering of my slavery, in honor of, and in union with, that subjection which the Eternal Wisdom deigned to have to thy maternity; in homage to the power which both of you have over this poor sinner, and in thanksgiving for the privileges with which the Holy Trinity has favored thee. I declare that I wish henceforth, as thy true slave, to seek thy honor and to obey thee in all things.

O admirable Mother, present me to thy dear Son as His eternal slave, so that as He has redeemed me by thee, by thee He may receive me! O Mother of mercy, grant me the grace to obtain the true Wisdom of God; and for that end receive me among those whom thou lovest and teachest, whom thou leadest, nourishest and protectest as thy children and thy slaves.

O faithful Virgin, make me in all things so perfect a disciple, imitator and slave of the Incarnate Wisdom, Jesus Christ thy Son, that I may attain, by thine intercession and by thine example, to the fullness of His age on earth and of His glory in Heaven. Amen.

Consecration to Mary by St. Maximillian Kolbe

O Immaculate, Queen of heaven and earth, Refuge of sinners and our most loving Mother, God has willed to entrust the entire order of mercy to You, I, an unworthy sinner, cast myself at Your feet, humbly imploring You to take me with all that I am and have, wholly to Yourself as Your possession and property. Please make of me, of all my powers of soul and body, of my whole life, death, and eternity, whatever pleases You. If it pleases You, use all that I am and have without reserve, wholly to accomplish what has been said of You: *"She will crush your head"*, and *"You alone have destroyed all heresies in the whole world."* Let me be a fit instrument in Your immaculate and most merciful hands for introducing and increasing Your glory to the maximum in all the many strayed and indifferent souls, and thus help extend as far as possible the blessed Kingdom of the Most Sacred Heart of Jesus. For, wherever You enter, You obtain the grace of conversion and sanctification, since it is through Your hands that all graces come to us from the Most Sacred Heart of Jesus.

V. Allow me to praise You, O most holy Virgin.

R. *Give me strength against Your enemies.*

St. Louis De Montfort's Prayer to Mary

Hail Mary, beloved Daughter of the Eternal Father! Hail Mary, admirable Mother of the Son! Hail Mary, faithful spouse of the Holy Ghost! Hail Mary, my dear Mother, my loving Mistress, my powerful sovereign! Hail my joy, my glory, my heart and my soul! Thou art all mine by mercy, and I am all thine by justice. But I am not yet sufficiently thine. I now give myself wholly to thee without keeping anything back for myself or others. If thou still seest in me anything which does not belong to thee, I beseech thee to take it and to make thyself the absolute Mistress of all that is mine. Destroy in me all that may be displeasing to God, root it up and bring it to naught; place and cultivate in me everything that is pleasing to thee.

May the light of thy faith dispel the darkness of my mind; may thy profound humility take the place of my pride; may thy sublime contemplation check the distractions of my wandering imagination; may thy continuous sight of God fill my memory with His presence; may the burning love of thy heart inflame the lukewarmness of mine; may thy virtues take the place of my sins; may thy merits be my only adornment in the sight of God and make up for all that is wanting in me. Finally, dearly beloved Mother, grant, if it be possible, that I may have no other spirit but thine to know Jesus and His divine will; that I may have no other soul but thine to praise and glorify the Lord; that I may have no other heart but thine to love God with a love as pure and ardent as thine I do not ask thee for visions, revelations, sensible devotion or spiritual pleasures. It is thy privilege to see God clearly; it is thy privilege to enjoy heavenly bliss; it is thy privilege to triumph gloriously in Heaven at the right hand of thy Son and to hold absolute sway over angels, men and demons; it is thy privilege to dispose of all the gifts of God, just as thou willest.

Such is, O heavenly Mary, the "best part," which the Lord has given thee and which shall never be taken away from thee--and this thought fills my heart with joy. As for my part here below, I wish for no other than that which was thine: to believe sincerely without spiritual pleasures; to suffer joyfully without human consolation; to die continually to myself without respite; and to work zealously and unselfishly for thee until death as the humblest of thy servants. The only grace I beg thee to obtain for me is that every day and every moment of my life I may say: Amen, So be it--to all that thou didst do while on earth; Amen, so be it--to all that thou art now doing in Heaven; Amen, so be it--to all that thou art doing in my soul, so that thou alone mayest fully glorify Jesus in me for time and eternity. Amen.

We Fly To Your Protection…

We fly to thy patronage, O holy Mother of God; despise not our petitions in our necessities, but deliver us always from all dangers, O glorious and blessed Virgin. Amen.

Loving Mother of the Redeemer

Loving Mother of the Redeemer, gate of heaven, star of the sea, assist your people who have fallen yet strive to rise again. To the wonderment of nature you bore your Creator, yet remained a virgin after as before. You who received Gabriel's joyful greeting, have pity on us poor sinners.

Ave Maria Stella

Hail, bright star of ocean, God's own Mother blest,
Ever sinless Virgin, Gate of heavenly rest.
Taking that sweet Ave, Which from Gabriel came,
Peace confirm within us, Changing Eva's name.
Break the captives' fetters, Light on blindness pour,
All our ills expelling, Every bliss implore.
Show thyself a Mother; May the Word Divine,
Born for us thy Infant, Hear our prayers through thine.

Virgin all excelling, Mildest of the mild,

Freed from guilt, preserve us, Pure and undefiled.

Keep our life all spotless, Make our way secure,

Till we find in Jesus, Joy forevermore.

Through the highest heaven, To the Almighty Three,

Father, Son and Spirit, One same glory be. Amen.

Litany of the Blessed Mother

Lord, have mercy on us. *Christ, have mercy on us.* Lord, have
mercy on us.

Christ hear us. *Christ, graciously hear us.*

God, the Father of heaven, *Have mercy on us.*

God, the Son, Redeemer of the world: *Have mercy on us.*

God, the Holy Ghost, *Have mercy on us.*

Holy Trinity, One God, *Have mercy on us.*

Holy Mary, *pray for us.* (repeat at end of each phrase.)

Holy Mother of God,

Holy Virgin of virgins,

Mother of Christ,

Mother of the Church,

Mother of Mercy,

Mother of divine grace,

Mother of Hope,

Mother most pure,

Mother most chaste,

Mother inviolate,

Mother undefiled,

Mother most amiable,

Mother admirable,

Mother of good counsel,

Mother of our Creator,

Mother of our Savior,

Virgin most prudent,

Virgin most venerable,

Virgin most renowned,

Virgin most powerful,

Virgin most merciful,

Virgin most faithful,

Mirror of justice,

Seat of wisdom,

Cause of our joy,

Spiritual vessel,

Vessel of honor,

Singular vessel of devotion,

Mystical rose,

Tower of David,

Tower if ivory,

House of gold,

Ark of the covenant,

Gate of heaven,

Morning star,

Health of the sick,

Refuge of sinners,

Solace of Migrants,

Comfort of the afflicted,

Help of Christians,

Queen of Angels,

Queen of Patriarchs,

Queen of Prophets,

Queen of Apostles,

Queen of Martyrs,

Queen of Confessors,

Queen of Virgins,

Queen of all Saints,

Queen conceived without original sin,

Queen assumed into heaven,

Queen of the most holy Rosary,

Queen of families,

Queen of peace.

Lamb of God, who takest away the sins of the world, *Spare us, O Lord.*

Lamb of God, who takest away the sins of the world, *Graciously hear us O Lord.*

Lamb of God, who takest away the sins of the world, *Have mercy on us.*

V. Pray for us, O holy Mother of God.

R. *That we may be made worthy of the promises of Christ.*

Let us pray:

Grant, O Lord God, we beseech Thee, that we Thy servants may rejoice in continual health of mind and body; and, through the glorious intercession of Blessed Mary ever Virgin, may be freed from present sorrow, and enjoy eternal gladness. Through Christ our Lord. Amen.

Chaplet of Sorrows

Chaplet of Sorrows for Priests

1 Our Father

1 Hail Mary

1 Creed

On each 'Our Father' bead of a rosary, say the Sorrow of Our Lady's Heart and a Hail Mary.

On each 'Hail Mary' bead of a rosary, say:

"O Sorrowful and Immaculate Heart of Mary, Pray for us who have recourse to Thee!"

After all 7 decades, say 1 'Glory Be', 'Hail Holy Queen' and 'Memorare'

(You can also add the 'Sabet Mater' if you would like.)

Seven Sorrows of Our Lady (each one is a 'Mystery' of the Chaplet)

1. First Sorrow of Our Lady's Heart is the Prophesy of Simeon

2. <u>Second Sorrow</u> of Our Lady's Heart is the Flight into Egypt

3. <u>Third Sorrow</u> of Our Lady's Heart is the Losing of the Child Jesus in the Temple

4. <u>Fourth Sorrow</u> of Our Lady's Heart is when Mary Meets Jesus on His Way to Calvary

5. <u>Fifth Sorrow</u> of Our Lady's Heart is when Jesus Dies on the Cross

6. <u>Sixth Sorrow</u> of Our Lady's Heart is when Jesus is Taken Down from the Cross and Laid in Her Arms (the 'Pieta')

7. <u>Seventh Sorrow</u> of Our Lady's Heart is when Jesus is Taken from Her Arms and Laid in the Tomb

<u>Chaplet of Our Lady's Tears</u>

(As given to Sister Amalia Aguirre (1901–1977) was a professed religious of the Missionaries of Jesus Crucified in Brazil.)

Beginning Prayer:

Crucified Jesus, prostrate at Your feet, we offer You the tears of the Mother who, with love full of devotion and sympathy, accompanied You on Your painful way to Calvary. Grant, O Good Master, that we take to heart the lessons which the tears of Your

Most Holy Mother have taught us, so that we may fulfill Your Holy Will on earth and become worthy to praise and bless You in heaven for all eternity. Amen.

Large Beads *(instead of the "Our Father" say)*:
v. O Jesus, behold the tears of the One who loved You most while on earth,
r. And who loves You most ardently in heaven.

Small Beads *(instead of the "Hail Mary" say seven (or ten) times)*:
v. O Jesus hear our prayers,
r. For the sake of the tears of Your most holy Mother.

At the End *(repeat 3 times)*:
v. O Jesus, behold the tears of the One who loved You most while on earth,
r. And who loves You most ardently in heaven.

Concluding Prayer:
O Mary, Mother of Love, Mother of Sorrows and Mother of Mercy, we beg You, join Your prayers with ours so that Jesus, Your Divine Son to whom we turn, will graciously hear our petitions for the sake of Your maternal tears, and, together with the graces we implore, grant us finally the reward of eternal life. Amen.
With Your tears, O sorrowful Mother, destroy the dominion of Satan. Through Your divine tenderness, O bound and fettered Jesus, defend the world from the errors which threaten it. Amen.

Stabat Mater

At the cross her station keeping
stood the mournful Mother weeping,
close to Jesus to the last.

Through her heart, His sorrow sharing,
all His bitter anguish bearing
now at length the sword had passed.

Oh, how sad and sore distressed
was that Mother highly blessed,
of the sole-begotten One!

Christ above in torment hangs,
she beneath beholds the pangs
of her dying, glorious Son.

Is there one who would not weep,
whelmed in miseries so deep,
Christ's dear Mother to behold?

Can the human heart refrain
from partaking in her pain,
in that Mother's pain untold?

Bruised, derided, cursed, defiled,
she beheld her tender Child
all with bloody scourges rent.

For the sins of His own nation,
saw Him hang in desolation,
till His spirit forth He sent.

O sweet Mother! fount of love!
Touch my spirit from above,
make my heart with thine accord.

Make me feel as thou hast felt;
make my soul to glow and melt
with the love of Christ, my Lord.

Holy Mother! pierce me through,
in my heart each wound renew
of my Savior crucified.

Let me share with thee His pain,
who for all our sins was slain,
who for me in torments died.

Let me mingle tears with thee,
mourning Him who mourned for me,
all the days that I may live.

By the Cross with thee to stay,
there with thee to weep and pray,
is all I ask of thee to give.

Virgin of all virgins blest!,
Listen to my fond request:
let me share thy grief divine;

Let me, to my latest breath,
in my body bear the death
of that dying Son of thine.

Wounded with His every wound,
steep my soul till it hath swooned,
in His very Blood away;

Be to me, O Virgin, nigh,
lest in flames I burn and die,
in His awful Judgment Day.

Christ, when Thou shalt call me hence,
be Thy Mother my defense,
be Thy Cross my victory;

While my body here decays,
may my soul Thy goodness praise,
safe in paradise with Thee. ***Amen.***

Litany of Our Lady of Consolation, St. Monica and St. Augustine

Lord have mercy on us. (*Christ have mercy on us.*) Lord have mercy on us.

Christ, hear us. Christ, *graciously hear us.*

God the Father of Heaven, *Have mercy on us.*

God the Son, Redeemer of the world, *Have mercy on us.*

God the Holy Ghost, *Have mercy on us.*

Holy Trinity, One God, *Have mercy on us.*

Mary, our Mother and the Mother of Jesus, *Pray for us.*

Mary, our Mother of Consolation, *Pray for us.*

Mary, the source of our hope, *Pray for us.*

Mary, the refuge of sinners, *Pray for us.*

Mary, the guiding star of our lives, *Pray for us.*

Mary, source of strength in our weakness, *Pray for us.*

Mary, source of light in our darkness, *Pray for us.*

Mary, source of consolation in our sorrows, *Pray for us.*

Mary, source of victory in our temptations, *Pray for us.*

Mary, who leads us to Jesus, *Pray for us.*

Mary, who keeps us with Jesus, *Pray for us.*

Mary, who redeems us through Jesus, *Pray for us.*

Mary, Mother of Consolation, our Patroness, *Pray for us.*

Saint Augustine, triumph of Divine grace, *Pray for us.*

St. Augustine, so faithful to grace, *Pray for us.*

St. Augustine, glowing with pure love of God, *Pray for us.*

St. Augustine, filled with zeal for God's glory, *Pray for us.*

St. Augustine, bright star in the firmament of the Church, *Pray for us.*

St. Augustine, so great and so humble, *Pray for us.*

St. Augustine, dauntless defender of the Faith, *Pray for us.*

St. Augustine, vanquisher of heresy, *Pray for us.*

St. Augustine, prince of bishops and doctors, *Pray for us.*

St. Augustine, our father, *Pray for us.*

Saint Monica, devout mother of St. Augustine, *Pray for us.*

St. Monica, whose prayers won Augustine from sin, *Pray for us.*

St. Monica, whose prayers gave Augustine to God, *Pray for us.*

St. Monica, pattern for wives, *Pray for us.*

St. Monica, model of mothers and mother of Saints, *Pray for us.*

St. Monica, exemplar of widows, *Pray for us.*

St. Monica, devoted to prayer, *Pray for us.*

St. Monica, so patient in trials, *Pray for us.*

St. Monica, so resigned in sorrow, *Pray for us.*

St. Monica, so happy in death, *Pray for us.*

St. Monica, devoted child of Mary, Mother of Consolation, *Pray for us.*

Lamb of God, Who takest away the sins of the world, *Spare us, O Lord.*

Lamb of God, Who takest away the sins of the world, *Graciously hear us, O Lord.*

Lamb of God, Who takest away the sins of the world, *Have mercy on us.*

V. Pray for us, O holy Mother of Consolation,

R. *That we may be made worthy of the promises of Christ.*

V. Pray for us, O holy father, Saint Augustine,

R. *That we may be made worthy of the promises of Christ.*

V. Pray for us, O holy mother, Saint Monica,

R. *That we may be made worthy of the promises of Christ.*

Let Us Pray.

O Lord Jesus Christ, Father of mercies and God of all consolation, grant propitiously to Thy servants that, joyfully venerating Thy most pure Mother Mary as Our Lady of Consolation we may be consoled by her in our sorrows, fortified in our trials through life, and in dying, may merit the ineffable consolations of Heaven for all eternity. Amen.

Consecration Prayer to Our Lady of the Miraculous Medal

(Can be prayed whenever needing big graces –and is often used as a 33 day novena from November 5th or 6th –December 8th (Solemnity of the Immaculate Conception of the Blessed Virgin Mary;) or as a 40

day novena from October 19- November 27, the Feast of Our Lady of the Miraculous Medal)

An Act of Consecration to Our Lady of the Miraculous Medal

O Virgin Mother of God, Mary Immaculate, we dedicate and consecrate ourselves to you under the title of Our Lady of the Miraculous Medal. May this Medal be for each one of us a sure sign of your affection for us and a constant reminder of our duties toward you. Ever while wearing it, may we be blessed by your loving protection and preserved in the grace of your Son. O most powerful Virgin, Mother of our Savior, keep us close to you every moment of our lives. Obtain for us, your children, the grace of a happy death; so that, in union with you, we may enjoy the bliss of heaven forever. Amen.

Repeat 3 times:

O Mary, conceived without sin –Pray for us who have recourse to you.

Miraculous Medal Novena Prayer

O Immaculate Virgin Mary, Mother of Our Lord Jesus and our Mother, penetrated with the most lively confidence in your all-powerful and never-failing intercession, manifested so often through the Miraculous Medal, we your loving and trustful children implore you to obtain for us the graces and favors we ask during this Novena, if they be beneficial to our immortal souls, and the souls for whom we pray.

(Here privately form your petitions.)

You know, O Mary, how often our souls have been the sanctuaries of your Son who hates iniquity. Obtain for us, then, a deep hatred of sin and that purity of heart which will attach us to God alone, so that our every thought, word and deed may tend to His greater glory. Obtain for us also a spirit of prayer and self-denial, that we may recover by penance what we have lost by sin and at length attain to that blessed abode where you are the Queen of angels and of men Amen.

Prayer to Our Lady, Undoer of Knots

Virgin Mary, Mother of fair love, Mother who never refuses to come to the aid of a child in need, Mother whose hands never cease to serve your beloved children because they are moved by the divine love and immense mercy that exists in your heart, cast your compassionate eyes upon me and see the snarl of knots that exist in my life.

You know very well how desperate I am, my pain and how I am bound by these knots.

Mary, Mother to whom God entrusted the undoing of the knots in the lives of His children, I entrust into your hands the ribbon of my life. No one, not even the evil one himself, can take it away from your precious care. In your hands there is no knot that cannot be undone. Powerful Mother, by your grace and intercessory power with Your Son and My Liberator, Jesus, take into your hands today this knot:

(insert your prayer request here)

I beg you to undo it for the glory of God, once for all, You are my hope.

O my Lady, you are the only consolation God gives me, the fortification of my feeble strength, the enrichment of my destitution and with Christ the freedom from my chains. Hear my plea. Keep me, guide me, protect me, o safe refuge!

Mary, Undoer of Knots, pray for me. Amen.

Prayer to Our Lady of Good Remedy

O Queen of Heaven and earth, most Holy Virgin, we venerate you. You are the beloved Daughter of the Most High God, the chosen Mother of the Incarnate Word, the Immaculate Spouse of the Holy Spirit, the Sacred Vessel of the Most Holy Trinity.

O Mother of the Divine Redeemer, who under the title of Our Lady of Good Remedy comes to the aid of all who call upon you, extend your maternal protection to us. We depend on you, Dear Mother, as helpless and needy children depend on a tender and caring mother.

Hail Mary, full of grace; the Lord is with thee; blessed art thou among women, and blessed is the fruit of thy womb, Jesus. Holy Mary, Mother of God, pray for us sinners, now and at the hour of our death. Amen.

O Lady of Good Remedy, source of unfailing help, grant that we may draw from your treasury of graces in our time of need.

Touch the hearts of sinners, that they may seek reconciliation and forgiveness. Bring comfort to the afflicted and the lonely; help the poor and the hopeless; aid the sick and the suffering. May they be healed in body and strengthened in spirit to endure their sufferings with patient resignation and Christian fortitude.

Hail Mary, full of grace; the Lord is with thee; blessed art thou among women, and blessed is the fruit of thy womb, Jesus. Holy Mary, Mother of God, pray for us sinners, now and at the hour of our death. Amen.

Dear Lady of Good Remedy, source of unfailing help, your compassionate heart knows a remedy for every affliction and misery we encounter in life. Help me with your prayers and intercession to find a remedy for my problems and needs, especially for . . .*(Mention your special intentions)*

On my part, O loving Mother, I pledge myself to a more intensely Christian lifestyle, to a more careful observance of the laws of God, to be more conscientious in fulfilling the obligations of my state in life, and to strive to be a source of healing in this broken world of ours.

Dear Lady of Good Remedy, be ever present to me, and through your intercession, may I enjoy health of body and peace of mind, and grow stronger in the faith and in the love of your Son, Jesus.

Hail Mary, full of grace; the Lord is with thee; blessed art thou among women, and blessed is the fruit of thy womb, Jesus. Holy Mary, Mother of God, pray for us sinners, now and at the hour of our death. Amen.

Pray for us, O Holy Mother of Good Remedy, -That we may deepen our dedication to your Son, and make the world alive with His Spirit.

Prayer to the Maria Bambina (Infant Mary)

Hail, Infant Mary, full of grace, the Lord is with thee, blessed art thou forever, and blessed are thy holy parents Joachim and Anne, of whom thou wast miraculously born. Mother of God, intercede for us.

We fly to thy patronage, holy and amiable Child Mary, despise not our prayers in our necessities, but deliver us from all dangers, glorious and blessed Virgin.

V. Pray for us, holy Child Mary.

R. That we may be made worthy of the promises of Christ.
Let us Pray: O almighty and merciful God, Who through the cooperation of the Holy Ghost, didst prepare the body and soul of the Immaculate Infant Mary that she might be the worthy Mother of Thy Son, and didst preserve her from all stain, grant that we who venerate with all our hearts her most holy childhood, may be freed, through her merits and intercession, from all uncleanness of mind and body, and be able to imitate her perfect humility, obedience and charity. Through Christ Our Lord. Amen.

Novena Prayer to the Maria Bambina (Infant Mary)

Holy Child Mary of the royal house of David, Queen of the
angels,
Mother of grace and love, I greet you with all my heart.
Obtain for me the grace to love the Lord faithfully during
all the days of my life. Obtain for me, too, a great devotion
to you, who are the first creature of God's love.

Hail Mary, full of grace...............

O heavenly Child Mary, who like a pure dove was born
immaculate and beautiful, true prodigy of the wisdom of
God, my soul rejoices in you. Oh! Do help me to preserve
the angelic virtue of purity at the cost of any sacrifice.

Hail Mary, full of grace...............

Hail, lovely and holy Child, spiritual garden of delight, where, on the day of the Incarnation, the tree of life was planted, assist me to avoid the poisonous fruit of vanity and pleasures of the world.

Help me to engraft into my soul the thoughts, feelings, and virtues of your divine Son.

Hail Mary, full of grace...............

Hail, admirable Child Mary, Mystical Rose, closed garden, open only to the heavenly Spouse. O Lily of paradise, make me love the humble and hidden life; let the heavenly Spouse find the gate of my heart always open to the loving calls of His graces and inspiration.

Hail Mary, full of grace...............

Holy Child Mary, mystical dawn, gate of heaven, you are my trust and hope.

O powerful advocate, from your cradle stretch out your hand, support me on the path of life.

Make me serve God with ardor and constancy until death and so reach an eternity with you.

Hail Mary, full of grace...............

Prayer:

Blessed Child Mary, destined to be the Mother of God and our loving Mother, by the heavenly graces you lavish upon us, mercifully listen to my supplications. In the needs which press upon me from every side and especially in my present tribulation, I place all my trust in you.

O holy Child, by the privileges granted to you alone and by the merits which you have acquired, show that the source of spiritual favors and the continuous benefits which you dispense are inexhaustible, because your power with the Heart of God is unlimited.

Deign through the immense profusion of graces with which the Most High has enriched you from the first moment of your Immaculate Conception, grant me, O Celestial Child, my petition, and I shall eternally praise the goodness of your Immaculate Heart.

IMPRIMATUR

In Curia Archiep. Mediolani

31 August 1931

Can. CAVEZZALI, Pro Vic. Gen

Litany in Honor of the Holy Infancy of The Blessed Virgin by St. John Eudes

Lord, have mercy on us,	*Lord, have mercy on us.*
Christ, have mercy on us,	*Christ, have mercy on us.*
Lord, have mercy on us,	*Lord, have mercy on us.*
Infant Jesus, hear us,	*Have mercy on us.*

Infant Jesus, graciously hear us,	*Have mercy on us.*
God the Father of heaven,	*Have mercy on us.*
God the Son, Redeemer of the World,	*Have mercy on us.*
God the Holy Ghost,	*Have mercy on us.*
Holy Infant Mary,	*Pray for us.*
Infant Daughter of the Father,	*Pray for us.*
Infant, Mother of the Son,	*Pray for us.*
Infant, Spouse of the Holy Ghost,	*Pray for us.*
Infant, fruit of the prayers of thy parents,	*Pray for us.*
Infant, Sanctuary of the Holy Trinity,	*Pray for us.*
Infant, riches of thy father,	*Pray for us.*
Infant, delight of thy mother,	*Pray for us.*
Infant, honor of thy father,	*Pray for us.*
Infant, honor of thy mother,	*Pray for us.*
Infant, miracle of nature,	*Pray for us.*
Infant, prodigy of grace,	*Pray for us.*
Immaculate in thy Conception,	*Pray for us.*
Most holy in thy Nativity,	*Pray for us.*
Most devout in thy Presentation,	*Pray for us.*
Masterpiece of God's grace,	*Pray for us.*
Aurora of the Sun of Justice,	*Pray for us.*
Beginning of our joy,	*Pray for us.*
End of our evils,	*Pray for us.*
Infant, joy of earth,	*Pray for us.*
Pattern of our charity,	*Pray for us.*
Model of our humility,	*Pray for us.*

Infant, most powerful,	*Pray for us.*
Infant, most mild,	*Pray for us.*
Infant, most pure,	*Pray for us.*
Infant, most obedient,	*Pray for us.*
Infant, most poor,	*Pray for us.*
Infant, most meek,	*Pray for us.*
Infant, most amiable,	*Pray for us.*
Infant, most admirable,	*Pray for us.*
Infant, incomparable,	*Pray for us.*
Infant, health of the sick,	*Pray for us.*
Comfortess of the afflicted,	*Pray for us.*
Refuge of Sinners,	*Pray for us.*
Hope of Christians,	*Pray for us.*
Lady of the Angels,	*Pray for us.*
Daughter of the Patriarchs,	*Pray for us.*
Desire of the Prophets,	*Pray for us.*
Mistress of the Apostles,	*Pray for us.*
Strength of Martyrs,	*Pray for us.*
Glory of the Priesthood,	*Pray for us.*
Joy of Confessors,	*Pray for us.*
Purity of Virgins,	*Pray for us.*
Queen of all Saints,	*Pray for us.*
Infant, our Mother,	*Pray for us.*
Infant, Queen of our hearts,	*Pray for us.*
Lamb of God, Who takest away the sins of the world,	*Spare us, Infant Jesus.*
	Graciously hear us,

Lamb of God, Who takest away the sins *Infant Jesus.*
of the world, *Have mercy on us, Infant*
Lamb of God, Who takest away the sins *Jesus.*
of the world, *Hear us.*
Infant Jesus, *Graciously hear us.*
Infant Jesus,

LET US PRAY

O almighty and merciful God, Who through the cooperation of the Holy Ghost, didst prepare the body and soul of the Immaculate Infant Mary that she might be the worthy Mother of Thy Son, and didst preserve her from all stain, grant that we who venerate with all our hearts her most holy childhood, may be freed, through her merits and intercession, from all uncleanness of mind and body, and be able to imitate her perfect humility, obedience and charity. Through Christ Our Lord. Amen.

Chapter 10

Sunday Prayers – to the Holy Name of Jesus

Litany of the Holy Name of Jesus

Lord, have mercy on us. *Christ, have mercy on us.* Lord, have mercy on us.

Jesus, hear us. *Jesus, graciously hear us.*

God the Father of Heaven *Have mercy on us.*

God the Son, Redeemer of the world, *Have mercy on us.*

God the Holy Spirit, *Have mercy on us.*

Holy Trinity, one God, *Have mercy on us.*

Jesus, Son of the living God, **Have mercy on us.**

Jesus, splendor of the Father, [*etc.*]

Jesus, brightness of eternal light.

Jesus, King of glory.

Jesus, sun of justice.

Jesus, Son of the Virgin Mary.

Jesus, most amiable.

Jesus, most admirable.

Jesus, the mighty God.

Jesus, Father of the world to come.

Jesus, angel of great counsel.

Jesus, most powerful.

Jesus, most patient.

Jesus, most obedient.

Jesus, meek and humble of heart.

Jesus, lover of chastity.

Jesus, lover of us.

Jesus, God of peace.

Jesus, author of life.

Jesus, example of virtues.

Jesus, zealous lover of souls.

Jesus, our God.

Jesus, our refuge.

Jesus, father of the poor.

Jesus, treasure of the faithful.

Jesus, good Shepherd.

Jesus, true light.

Jesus, eternal wisdom.

Jesus, infinite goodness.

Jesus, our way and our life.

Jesus, joy of Angels.

Jesus, King of the Patriarchs.

Jesus, Master of the Apostles.

Jesus, teacher of the Evangelists.

Jesus, strength of Martyrs.

Jesus, light of Confessors.

Jesus, purity of Virgins.

Jesus, crown of Saints.

V. Be merciful, *R. spare us, O Jesus.*

V. Be merciful, *R. graciously hear us, O Jesus.*

V. From all evil, *R. deliver us, O Jesus.*

From all sin, **deliver us, O Jesus.**

From Your wrath, [*etc.*]

From the snares of the devil.

From the spirit of fornication.

From everlasting death.

From the neglect of Your inspirations.

By the mystery of Your holy Incarnation.

By Your Nativity.

By Your Infancy.

By Your most divine Life.

By Your labors.

By Your agony and passion.

By Your cross and dereliction.

By Your sufferings.

By Your death and burial.

By Your Resurrection.

By Your Ascension.

By Your institution of the most Holy Eucharist.

By Your joys.

By Your glory.

V. Lamb of God, who takest away the sins of the world,

R. *spare us, O Jesus.*

V. Lamb of God, who takest away the sins of the world,

R. *graciously hear us, O Jesus.*

V. Lamb of God, who takest away the sins of the world,

R. *have mercy on us, O Jesus.*

V. Jesus, hear us.

R. *Jesus, graciously hear us.*

Let us pray:

O Lord Jesus Christ, You have said, "Ask and you shall receive, seek, and you shall find, knock, and it shall be opened to you." Grant, we beg of You, to us who ask it, the gift of Your most divine love, that we may ever love You with our whole heart, in word and deed, and never cease praising You.

Give us, O Lord, as much a lasting fear as a lasting love of Your Holy Name, for You, who live and are King for ever and ever, never fail to govern those whom You have solidly established in Your love. Amen.

Chapter 11

Extra Prayers

Chaplet of Divine Mercy

St. Faustina's Prayer for Sinners

O Jesus, eternal Truth, our Life, I call upon You and I beg Your mercy for poor sinners. O sweetest Heart of my Lord, full of pity and unfathomable mercy, I plead with You for poor sinners. O Most Sacred Heart, Fount of Mercy from which gush forth rays of inconceivable graces upon the entire human race, I beg of You light for poor sinners. O Jesus, be mindful of Your own bitter

Passion and do not permit the loss of souls redeemed at so dear a price of Your most precious Blood. O Jesus, when I consider the great price of Your Blood, I rejoice at its immensity, for one drop alone would have been enough for the salvation of all sinners. Although sin is an abyss of wickedness and ingratitude, the price paid for us can never be equaled. Therefore, let every soul trust in the Passion of the Lord, and place its hope in His mercy. God will not deny His mercy to anyone. Heaven and earth may change, but God's mercy will never be exhausted. Oh, what immense joy burns in my heart when I contemplate Your incomprehensible goodness, O Jesus! I desire to bring all sinners to Your feet that they may glorify Your mercy throughout endless ages *(Diary of Saint Maria Faustina Kowalska, 72)*.

You expired, Jesus, but the source of life gushed forth for souls, and the ocean of mercy opened up for the whole world. O Fount of Life, unfathomable Divine Mercy, envelop the whole world and empty Yourself out upon us.

(Repeat three times)

O Blood and Water, which gushed forth from the Heart of Jesus as a fount of mercy for us, I trust in You!

Our Father... Hail Mary... Apostle's Creed

1.) **In remembrance of the Crown of Thorns He wore on His Head and around His Heart and the wounds they caused we pray...**

(On 'Our Father Beads…) Eternal Father, I offer you the Body and Blood, Soul and Divinity of Your Dearly Beloved Son, Our Lord, Jesus Christ, in atonement for our sins and those of the whole world.

(On 'Hail Mary' Beads…) For the sake of His sorrowful Passion, have mercy on us and on the whole world. (Repeat 10 times…)

2.) In remembrance of the wound in His Shoulder and from the Scourging we pray…

(On 'Our Father Beads…) Eternal Father, I offer you the Body and Blood, Soul and Divinity of Your Dearly Beloved Son, Our Lord, Jesus Christ, in atonement for our sins and those of the whole world.

(On 'Hail Mary' Beads…) For the sake of His sorrowful Passion, have mercy on us and on the whole world. (Repeat 10 times…)

3.) In remembrance of the wounds in His Hands we pray…
(On 'Our Father Beads…) Eternal Father, I offer you the Body and Blood, Soul and Divinity of Your Dearly Beloved Son, Our Lord, Jesus Christ, in atonement for our sins and those of the whole world.

(On 'Hail Mary' Beads…) For the sake of His sorrowful Passion, have mercy on us and on the whole world. (Repeat 10 times…)

4.) In remembrance of the wounds in His Feet we pray...

(On 'Our Father Beads...) Eternal Father, I offer you the Body and Blood, Soul and Divinity of Your Dearly Beloved Son, Our Lord, Jesus Christ, in atonement for our sins and those of the whole world.

(On 'Hail Mary' Beads...) For the sake of His sorrowful Passion, have mercy on us and on the whole world. (Repeat 10 times...)

5.) In remembrance of the wound in His Side, from whence Blood and Water poured forth as a fountain of Mercy upon the entire world we pray...

(On 'Our Father Beads...) Eternal Father, I offer you the Body and Blood, Soul and Divinity of Your Dearly Beloved Son, Our Lord, Jesus Christ, in atonement for our sins and those of the whole world.

(On 'Hail Mary' Beads...) For the sake of His sorrowful Passion, have mercy on us and on the whole world. (Repeat 10 times...)

THREE TIMES: Holy God, Holy Mighty One, Holy Immortal One, have mercy on us and on the whole world.

(Repeat three times)

O Blood and Water, which gushed forth from the Heart of Jesus as a fountain of mercy for us, I trust in You!

Jesus, I trust in You.

Jesus, I trust in You.

Jesus, King of my heart, I trust in You.

<u>Closing Prayers</u>

Eternal God, in whom mercy is endless and the treasury of compassion — inexhaustible, look kindly upon us and increase Your mercy in us, that in difficult moments we might not despair nor become despondent, but with great confidence submit ourselves to Your holy will, which is Love and Mercy itself.

O Greatly Merciful God, Infinite Goodness, today all mankind calls out from the abyss of its misery to Your mercy — to Your compassion, O God; and it is with its mighty voice of misery that it cries out. Gracious God, do not reject the prayer of this earth's exiles! O Lord, Goodness beyond our understanding, Who are acquainted with our misery through and through, and know that by our own power we cannot ascend to You, we implore You: anticipate us with Your grace and keep on increasing Your mercy in us, that we may faithfully do Your holy will all through our life and at death's hour. Let the omnipotence of Your mercy shield us from the darts of our salvation's enemies, that we may with confidence, as Your children, await Your [Son's] final coming — that day known to You alone. And we expect to obtain everything promised us by Jesus in spite of all our wretchedness. For Jesus is our Hope: through His merciful Heart, as through an open gate, we pass through to heaven (*Diary*, 1570).

Jesus, meek and humble of Heart, make our hearts like unto Thine!

Simple Deliverance Prayer

Lord, almighty, merciful and omnipotent God,

Father, Son and Holy Spirit,

Drive out from me all influence of evil spirits.

Father, in the name of Christ, I plead you to break any chain that the devil has on me.

Pour upon me the most precious blood of your Son.

May His immaculate and redeeming blood break all bonds of my body or mind.

I ask you this through the intercession of the Most Holy Virgin Mary.

Archangel St. Michael, intercede and come to my help.

In the name of Jesus I command all devils that could have any influence over me,

To leave me forever.

By His scourging, His crown of thorns, His cross,

By His blood and Resurrection, I command all evil spirits to leave me.

By the True God

By the Holy God

By God who can do all,

I command you, filthy demon, to leave me in the name of Jesus, my Savior and Lord.

Prayer For the Deliverance of Homes

Heavenly Father, I/We acknowledge you as the Lord of heaven and earth. You are the creator of everything. Thank you for your Son, Lord Jesus Christ, His death, resurrection and ascension. Thank you for our family, all our relationships, our home, property, ministry and possessions. I/We claim our family, relationships, homes/property, ministries and possessions as spiritual refuges and places of safety and protection against all attacks from Satan and his minions. In the name of the Lord Jesus Christ, the Eternal High Priest, I ask you to release His full power and authority through the Holy Spirit over us, our families, homes, properties, ministries, places of work and possessions.

Through the intercession of Mary, St. Michael, (… list your patron Saints…), St. Catherine of Sienna and Padre Pio I ask you Father in the Name of Your Son Jesus Christ, the Eternal High Priest with whom we share a one flesh union through our Baptism and reception of His Holy Body, Blood, Soul and Divinity in the Eucharist, to bind and cast away all evil spirits, unclean spirits, spirits not of God and any other spirits claiming ground on our persons, in our families, between all relationships, within our homes or lands, possessions and ministries based on previous relationships and ownership. Once you bind them, please cast them out from this home, family, relationships, property, ministries, neighborhood, our work places, possessions, bodies and souls and send them to the foot of the cross for Jesus Christ to deal with. In the name of the Lord Jesus Christ, I beg you Merciful and All-Omnipotent Father, to cancel any curses, commands or contracts exerting control, influence or access that they have formerly claimed against our family, relationships, home, this property and land, our ministry, work and possessions. I beg you to bind all interplay, interaction and communication of evil spirits, all blinding and binding and blocking spirits over our family, relationships, this place of prayer, our home, property, cars, workplaces, ministries and possessions. In the name of the Lord Jesus Christ, I beg you to send St Michael to cast them from these premises immediately. As they flee prevent them from exercising any vengeance or retaliation against the members of our families, relationships, homes, properties, ministries or possessions.

In the name of the Lord Jesus Christ, the Eternal High Priest and Eternal Exorcist, we beg you Holy Father to send upon us the Finger of God -the Holy Spirit -to cast out any evil influencing us, our relationships, faith, home, property, ministries or possessions and to pour forth the Holy Spirit in fullness with all His gifts, virtues and graces to preserve, protect and guide us and to enhance our spiritual gifts. And we ask the intercession of our holy guardian angels as well. Jesus, we trust in You! Mary, we are consecrated to you and we ask you to open the fullness of grace that comes from our consecration.

Anima Christi

Soul of Christ, sanctify me; Body of Christ, save me; Blood of Christ, inebriate me; Water from the side of Christ, wash me; Passion of Christ, strengthen me; O good Jesus, hear me; within your wounds, hide me; let me never be separated from you; from the evil one, protect me; at the hour of my death, call me; and bid me to come to you; that with your saints, I may praise you forever and ever. Amen.

Prayer for healing of the Family

Heavenly Father, I come before you as your child, in great need of your help; I have physical health needs, emotional needs, spiritual needs, and interpersonal needs. Many of my problems have been caused by my own failures, neglect and sinfulness, for which I humbly beg your forgiveness, Lord. But I also ask you to forgive the sins of my ancestors whose failures have left their effects on me in the form of unwanted tendencies, behavior patterns and defects in body, mind and spirit. Heal me, Lord, of all these disorders.

With your help I sincerely forgive everyone, especially living or dead members of my family tree, who have directly offended me or my loved ones in any way, or those whose sins have resulted in our present sufferings and disorders. In the name of your divine Son, Jesus, and in the power of his Holy Spirit, I ask you, Father, to deliver me, my entire family tree, all of my relationships and all those for whom I pray for from the influence of the evil one. Free all living and dead members of my family tree, including those in adoptive relationships, those in extended family relationships and those in friendships from every contaminating form of bondage. By your loving concern for us, heavenly Father, and by the shed Blood of your precious Son, Jesus, I beg you to extend your blessing to me, to all my living and deceased relatives and to all for whom we pray. Heal every negative effect transmitted through all past generations, and prevent such negative effects in future generations of my family tree.

I symbolically place the Cross of Jesus with His Most Precious Blood over the head and upon the heart of each person in my family tree, between each relationship and between each generation; I ask you to let the cleansing Blood of Jesus purify the bloodlines in my family lineage. Set your protective angels to encamp around us, and permit Archangel Raphael, the patron of healing, to administer your divine healing power to all of us, even in areas of genetic disability. Give special power to our family members' guardian angels to heal, protect, guide and encourage each of us in all our needs. Let your healing power be released at this very moment, and let it continue as long as your sovereignty permits.

In our family tree, Lord, replace all bondage with a holy bonding in family love. And let there be an ever-deeper bonding with you, Lord, by the Holy Spirit, to your Son, Jesus. Let the family of the

Holy Trinity pervade our family with its tender, warm, loving presence, so that our family may recognize and manifest that love in all our relationships. All of our unknown needs we include with this petition that we pray in Jesus' precious Name. Amen.

St. Joseph, Patron of family life, pray for us. Our Lady Queen of Peace, pray for us.

Prayer for the Consecration of the Family

Most Sacred Hearts of Jesus and Mary, I consecrate myself and my whole family to you. We consecrate to you our very being and all our life; all that we are, all that we have, and all that we love. To you we give our bodies, our hearts, and our souls. To you we dedicate our home and our country.

Mindful of this consecration, we now promise you to live the Christian way by the practice of Christian virtues, without regard for other's human opinion or respect. O most Sacred Hearts of Jesus and Mary, accept our humble confidence and this act of consecration by which we entrust ourselves and all our family to you. In you, we put all our hope, and we shall never be confounded.

Most holy Hearts of Jesus and Mary, united in perfect love, as you look upon us with mercy and caring, we consecrate our hearts, our lives, our family to you.

We know the beautiful example of your home in Nazareth was meant to be a model for each of our families. We hope to have, with your help, the unity and strong, enduring love you gave to one another.

May our home be filled with joy. May sincere affection, patience, tolerance and mutual respect be freely given to all. May our prayers be filled with the needs of others, not just ourselves and may we always be close to your sacraments.

Bless those who are present, as well as those who are absent, both the living and the dead; may peace be among us and when we are tested, grant us the Christian acceptance of God's will. Keep our family close to your Hearts; may your special protection be with us always. Most Sacred Hearts of Jesus and Mary, hear our prayer.

Most Sacred Heart of Jesus, have mercy on us.

Immaculate Heart of Mary, be our salvation. Amen.

Prayer to St. Rita

O glorious St. Rita, your pleadings before the divine crucifix have been known to grant favors that many would call the impossible. Lovely St. Rita, so humble, so pure, so devoted in your love for thy crucified Jesus, speak on my behalf for my petition which seems so impossible from my humbled position. *(Here mention your request).* Be propitious, O glorious St. Rita, to my petition, showing thy power with God on behalf of thy supplicant. Be lavish to me, as thou has been in so many wonderful cases for the greater glory of God. I promise, dear St. Rita, if my petition is granted, to glorify thee, by making known thy favor, to bless and sing thy praises forever. Relying then upon thy merits and power before the Sacred Heart of Jesus I pray. Amen.

Prayer to St. Jude

Most Holy Apostle St. Jude Thaddeus, faithful servant and friend of Jesus, the name of the traitor who delivered your beloved Master into the hands of the enemies has caused you to be forgotten by many, but the Church honors and invokes you universally as the patron of hopeless cases and of things despaired of. Pray for me who am so needy; make use, I implore you of that particular privilege accorded to you to bring visible and speedy help where help is almost despaired. Come to my assistance in this great need that I may receive the consolations and succor of heaven in all my necessities, tribulations, and sufferings particularly (*here mention your petition*) and that I may bless God with you and all the elect throughout eternity. I promise you, O blessed Jude to be ever mindful of this great favor, and I will never cease to honor you as my special and powerful patron and to do all in my power to encourage devotion to you. Amen.

Prayer to St. Philomena

O faithful virgin and glorious martyr, St. Philomena, who works so many miracles on behalf of the poor and sorrowing, have pity on me. Thou knowest the multitude and diversity of my needs. Behold me at thy feet, full of misery, but full of hope. I entreat thy charity, O great saint! Graciously hear me and obtain from God a favorable answer to the request which I now humbly lay before thee ... *(Here mention your petition.)* I am firmly convinced that through thy merits, through the scorn, the sufferings and the death thou didst endure, united to the merits of the Passion and death of Jesus, thy Spouse, I shall obtain what I ask of thee, and in the joy of my heart I will bless God, who is admirable in His saints. Amen. St. Philomena, powerful with God, pray for us.

Prayer for Protection Against Storms

(where you see the cross, make the Sign of the Cross)
Jesus Christ the King of Glory has come in Peace. +
God became man, +
and the Word was made flesh. +
Christ was born of a virgin. +
Christ suffered. +
Christ was crucified. +
Christ died. +
Christ rose from the dead. +
Christ ascended into Heaven. +

Christ conquers. +

Christ reigns. +

Christ orders. +

May Christ protect us from all storms and lightning. +

Christ went through their midst in Peace, +

and the Word was made Flesh. +

Christ is with us with Mary. +

Flee you enemy spirits because the Lion of the Generation of Juda, the Root of David, has won. +

Holy God! +

Holy Powerful God ! +

Holy Immortal God! +

Have mercy on us. Amen!

Cardinal John Henry Newman Prayer

(Mother Teresa prayed this prayer daily)

Dear Jesus, help me to spread Your fragrance wherever I go.

Flood my soul with Your spirit and life.

Penetrate and possess my whole being so utterly, that my life may only be a radiance of Yours.

Shine through me, and be so in me that every soul I come in contact with may feel Your presence in my soul.

Let them look up and see no longer me, but only Jesus!

Stay with me and then I shall begin to shine as You shine, so to shine as to be a light to others.

The light, O Jesus, will be all from You; none of it will be mine.

It will be You shining on others through me.

Let me thus praise You the way You love best, by shining on those around me.

Let me preach You without preaching, not by words but by my example, by the catching force of the sympathetic influence of what I do, the evident fullness of the love my heart bears to You.

Amen.

Chapter 12

Daily Prayers Written by Mary Kloska

Novena for Miraculous Graces

Mary Kloska –August 22, 2014

Dearest Mother, my Lady of Czestochowa, Our little Mother of Guadalupe, Immaculate Mother of Sorrows, Prayerful Mother of Carmel, our Pilgrim Lady of Fatima, Lourdes, La Salette, Medjugorje, Kibeho, our Lady clothed with the sun, my Hope of Perpetual Help, Good Remedy and Consolation, Our Lady, Undoer of Knots, my Queen of peace, I ask for You to take my heart (name other's –the hearts of all of my family –both physical and spiritual) and the hearts of all those who Your Son desires to help me on the way of my vocation and I ask you to place them within the divine Light of the Holy Spirit's presence within Your Own Heart –and to give them to Jesus. Please ask Him to take our hearts and to pray over them each individually in a special way during this 9 day novena –remaking them, recreating and transforming them as He sees fit –to be identical to the hearts He desired for us to hold within our beings *from the beginning* –full of the Father's fresh breath of Love, Life, Humility, Holiness, Silence, Wisdom, Knowledge, Understanding, Patience, Courage, Temperance, Prudence, Fortitude, Kindness, Gentleness, Strength, Piety, Purity, Peace, Hope, Faith and Love. Mary our Mother, I ask You to hold our hearts under the fountain of Love and Mercy that flows in Jesus' Blood and Water, Tears and Sweat, Fiat and Look, Forgiveness and Understanding, Hope and Trust –from each and every wound on His holy Body on the Cross, and most especially from His Heart. Just as His gift of redemption to us was concrete and physical in and through His body –I pray that it also touches and changes our minds, emotions, memory, psychology, spirit, soul and heart. May this redemption fall upon us through Jesus' breath –from on the Cross, in the Eucharist, and which you felt as He spoke to you resurrected. I ask that each of us is changed (healed, converted, enlightened and filled with perfect purity, wisdom, peace, surrender, courage, holiness, humility, silence and love) in these 9 days I consecrate to your Immaculate Herat, Jesus' Sacred Heart and Blood and to the Holy Spirit through your intercession. No prayer asked through your intercession, my Mother, or through the power of Jesus' most holy wounds and in His Name will be ignored or denied by our Good Father in Heaven. And so please beg Jesus for me, my Mother, that He places His wounded Hands upon each of us –especially our hearts –and to pray for us to the Father and to heal, fill, convert, and transform us completely to be little images of you and the intimate love you share with Him. I ask Him, my Crucified Husband and Lord, to say the powerful words He so often said on earth when He prayed for those who asked His help: **'Be done, be healed, be delivered, be changed, be filled, be protected, be blessed –I want it, according to My Father's will!'** I ask to be one heart with Him, as a Siamese identical twin –united as Husband and wife in human and divine perfect Love. I especially ask for the seemingly impossible graces that burn in my heart.

Mary, my Mother, I thank you for your beautiful, maternal and big sisterly Love. I re-consecrate my life and vocation to your Heart, and to Jesus' most precious, wounded Heart on the Cross. I ask Him to fill my fiat with His Father's Holy Will and His Spirit's powerful presence and to make all in my vocation, life, my family's lives, my spiritual children's lives be fulfilled perfectly according to His will. I give you everything, Jesus –through Mary. And I praise and thank You for Your perfect, never-ending, faithful Love. Please, set the fire of Your Love and Life in my vocation again – now and always. Help me trust in You! And help me receive ALL of Your Love! Jesus, have Mercy on us! Jesus, I trust in You! Mary, Queen of heaven and earth, pray for us!

His Faithful Love

September 1 (?) 2005

O little bread
O silent passion
Be the source of my quiet life
O raging fire
Flood of Blood
Enter me and cleanse my life
As I sit and drink from You
Fountain of Love and source of strength
Water me with Your rain of blood
Be my rest and empty me.
Hidden Love, broken Heart
Bright light of truth, please fill me
May your whiteness take my all
Share your darkness with me
Quiet passion, raging fire
Crying fiat in the night
Cry Your passion in my heart
Live your Cross within my life
May Your Heartbeat be my footsteps
May You breathe within my lungs
May I die in empty abandon
So You may carry me in Your Love. Amen. Alleluia

****

I want to live in the Garden of His Wounds.

I give You my soul, Jesus, as a place for You to rest Your soul, sorrowful unto death in the Garden of Olives.

I come to You as Your weak beloved wife, to calm Your pain and suffering by the presence of my quiet love.

I give You my nothingness, for You to fill with the empty nothingness You suffered on the Cross –May You fill my emptiness with the abyss of Your weary Heart's pain.

May You enter my body and take me as Your comfort, as Your wife, to Yourself in our union of spousal Love.

May my whole being be a gift to You,

May my whole life be a bed where You can find rest.

May my heart be always open to receive You.

May my heart be Your home, where You dwell with me in Love, just as Your Heart is my home, with You here on earth and forever in heaven. Amen. Fiat.

October, 2008

Lord, please give me Your Faith in the darkness,

Your Hope in the confusion,

Your Love and Trust in the face of evil,

Your thanksgiving in suffering,

Your pure, simple, little Heart in the midst of a world that has forgotten You.

Grant me light to see Your way for me,
silence to listen to Your will for me,
strength, courage and grace to fulfill Your Heart's desire for my life.

Possess me with Your holiness,
Capture me in Your humility,
Calm me with Your never-ending peace.
Help me to be the woman You created me to be –a child of Your Father, a spouse of Your Spirit, Your Heart, Jesus, ripped open as a fountain of mercy for the world upon the Cross.
Keep me faithful in darkness,
focused on You in confusion,
and cut the ties of my heart, mind, body and soul with the world, replacing them with bonds of Your Holy Love.

Help me to be Your Heart beating,
Your breath breathing,
Your eyes gazing,
Your ears receiving,
And Your mouth speaking –in silent union with You in this world.

I offer You my hands, feet, mouth –body, mind, emotions, memory, soul, works, breaths, sleep, fiat –my entire life and death –to union with You crucified.

May I always be Your little wife of crucified, fiat Love every moment of my existence here on earth and forever with You in the never-ending joy of union with You in eternity.

I wrap this consecration in the mantle of Your Mother's Love for Her to give You on my behalf.

O sweet Jesus, I trust in You. Amen.

Wise and Holy Mother…

September, 2009

Wise and Holy Mother, Virgin of Truth and Light,

Purity of love and faithfulness, trust and fiat in the great night of solitude, suffering and the Cross,

Please come and be with me now.

With the purity of your Love stain me.

With the wisdom of your heart, fill me.

With the Love that fires you as one with Jesus –enflame me.

With your faithful trust and endurance –hold me.

Help me to be who God created me to be… to please Him in all things I do, all moments of my life, in all thoughts, words, feelings, desires –in all my breath, life, love and death. Help me always in every moment to know, love and live His will all the days of my life.

Help me to be little in His loving arms and to trust regardless of the darkness.

Help me to live as His beloved wife –as He has called me to be.

Help me to be one with His wounded Heart –loving Him in pain and crucified one with Him in Love.

Strip the world from me.

Strip myself from me.

Help only Jesus and His Love, His Life and His death live within me –day and night.

Help me live my vocation as He desires.

Keep me open, keep me docile, keep me faithful as He was all the days of His life, but especially on the Cross.

Help me to love Him more –to complain less –to fiat more in trust.

I give you all of myself to give to Him again this day –all my thoughts, emotions, body, spirit, heart, soul, memory, wounds, temptations, sin and gifts and especially all of my relationships. Please heal what He desires to heal. Help me to believe and trust in His promises. Help me to love more than fear and fiat even when I fall. Make me into His true little wife crucified… help me to imitate your heart in virtues and His Heart in holy love.

I give you my nothing, I give you my darkness, I give you my abandonment, I give you my pain, I give you my confusion, I give you my blindness, I give you my failed love and I ask you to unite it with Him on the Cross so somehow my life has meaning to Him, even if this is all hidden from me.

I ask you, Mother of Sorrows, to give me all answers I need to questions, all graces I need to do His will and all healing I need so I can love as He desires. I specifically ask you in these 9 days for the special graces of *(mention your intention)*.

I ask you, Mother of Sorrows, to guide me personally –I ask for all the gifts that Jesus desires to give me (and for Him to take all He thinks best for me.)

Mother of Sorrows, help me to be the little wife crucified (victim of love and mercy) that Jesus has asked me to be with Him. Help me be as one with Him as the Father desires, in the Holy Spirit… I fall into your arms of love. I am His and so, I am also yours. Amen. +

April 23, 2010 –A New Prayer:

Jesus, please help me to:

Have **praying eyes** today –may my every look be a prayer of love and blessing and thanksgiving and praise.

Have **praying ears** today –may all I listen to be brought immediately into my heart's furnace of divine love and lost –as I offer it to Jesus on the Cross, dwelling within.

Have a **praying mouth** today –may all I speak touch others with the Holy Spirit in some way, offering them His peace, hope, wisdom and joy.

Have praying taste and smell today –may I crave only the love of God, may all that enters my mouth be in obedience to God, and may the Holy Spirit help me to offer many sacrifices of taste and food for the salvation of many souls.

Have **praying touch** today –may each person I encounter, each step, each movement be filled with the Holy Spirit and be done as a prayer of love, in a gentle, soft manner (as the Blessed Mother) so as to offer her heavenly peace to those around me.

Amen.

Litany of the Heart of Jesus

Heart of Jesus –be my home
Heart of Jesus -be my bed
        -be my covers
        -be my altar
        -be my church
        -be my school
        -be my food and drink
        -be my money and possession
        -be my warmth and clothes
        -be my defense
        -be my security
        -be my sense of life
        -be my answer
        -be my family
        -be my mother, my father, my brother and sister
        -be my little child
        -be my priest

-be my teacher

-be my healer

-be my Husband

-be my Beloved

-be my Savior

-be my God

-be my answer

-be all I need and all I have

-be my music, my color, my beauty

-be my light

-be my path

-be my truth and my guide

-be my wisdom

-be my future

-be a fire of Love and a cool paschal rain in me

-be a wind of peace in me

-be faithful in me

-be deep in me

-be free in me

-trust in me

-empty me

-beat in me

-act in me

-rest in me

Oh Heart of Jesus...

-breathe in me

-sleep in me

-speak in me

-hope in me

-believe in me

-forgive in me

-live in me

-be wounded in me

-be dark in me

-be alone in me

-be scourged, crowned with thorns and mocked in
me

-be crucified in me

-suffer in me

-resurrect in me

-hunger in me

-thirst in me

-be naked in me

-be filled in me

-be poor in me

-be humble in me

-be pure in me

-obey in me

-dance in me

-be gentle in me

-be courageous in me

-be tender in me

-be patient in me

-be delicate in me

-be silent in me

-purify me

-heal in me

-touch others in me

-watch in me

-desire in me

-fiat in me

-love in me

-play in me

-think in me

-fight all temptations in me

-erase all doubt in me

-feel in me

-remember in me

-be little in me

-be strong in me

-be firm in me

-be docile in me

-be open in me

Heart of Jesus –wait in me

-cry in me

-listen in me

-answer in me

-rejoice in me

-sing alleluia in me

-worship in me

-praise the Father in me

-glorify Him in me

-pray in me

-move in me

-unite with me

-know in me

-quiet me

-be full of the Spirit in me

-be one with Your Father's will in me

-make me Your little wife on the Cross

Oh sweet Heart of Jesus, please trust in me!

-be little and humble in me!

-suffer and die in me!

-love and fiat and fiat and Love in me!!

Oh Amen, alleluia, amen.

Chapter 13

Meditations on the Mysteries of the Rosary

Joyful Mystery of the Rosary

(*Monday and Saturday*)

First Mystery: The Annunciation of the Lord to Mary

In this mystery, we remember Our Lady's great Fiat –Her surrender to God and His plan –and we ask for the grace to say 'Fiat' to God along with her. We ask for docility of heart, for trust and for a great 'Yes' to God with our lives.

Second Mystery: The Visitation of Mary to Elizabeth

In this mystery, we see how not only Mary said 'Yes' to God in the Annunciation to receive Jesus into Her Womb and Heart, but also how She did not keep this gift for Herself. In this mystery Mary was the Great Tabernacle, like a Monstrance, carrying Baby Jesus to St. Elizabeth. And they spoke in such a way that their eyes, minds and hearts were centered on God. Our Lady prayed the Magnificat as St. John the Baptist (a little embryo in the womb of St. Elizabeth) was baptized by Jesus' presence in Mary. She prayed, '*My soul proclaims –magnifies –the Lord and my spirit rejoices in God, my Savior. For He has looked in great mercy on my lowliness –and henceforth all generations shall call me blessed. For the Mighty One has done great things for me, and Holy is His Name...*" In this mystery we pray that we, too, may carry Christ our Light to those around us and that our lives may always *'magnify the Lord.'*

Third Mystery: The Birth of Baby Jesus in Bethlehem

In this mystery we see the great poverty of Baby Jesus –already rejected by the world and born in a stable fit for animals. And yet the angels came to adore Him in song –the poor shepherds and the wise men came to give Him homage. And Mary and Joseph knelt over this tiny Child (our Eucharistic Bread of Life lying in a manger) with such prayerful devotion that heaven seemed to stand in awe. In this mystery, we pray for the humble poverty of spirit that the Holy Family encompassed in Bethlehem. And we ask for deeper love, adoration and devotion to His little Eucharistic Heart.

Fourth Mystery: The Presentation of our Lord Jesus in the Temple

In this mystery, we begin to see the price of Our Lady's Fiat. Here, She and Joseph present Baby Jesus in the Temple and are already told about the great sufferings He will endure *"This child will be for the rise and fall of many people –a sign to be contradicted –and you (His Mother) a sword will pierce so that the hearts of many souls may be revealed."* The 'Fiat' that Our Lady gave in the

Annunciation is repeated in the Temple –to the degree that She loves Her Son and to the degree that they are united (in flesh and in God) is the degree to which she will suffer. Love unites –you suffer to the degree you love and holy love increases as the suffering increases. In this mystery, we ask for the graces that Mary and Joseph had to continue in 'Fiat' to the mysterious plan of God that includes suffering in the life of Baby Jesus and in their own lives as well. And we pray that with them we may keep Christ as the center of our lives and hearts, *pondering these things in our hearts* with Him.

Fifth Mystery: Finding of the Child Jesus in the Temple

In this mystery, we see an example of humility in the priesthood –priests allowing themselves to be taught by a Child! We also see a great example of steadfastness in Jesus, willing to follow the Father's will –regardless of the cost (even if it causes the pain of confusion to His parents who He loved). We see Our Lady and Joseph willing to endure the loss both of their child and their God –in the midst of misunderstanding –and continually reaching forth for answers as to God's will for their lives. They searched, they questioned, they accepted and they pondered. In this mystery, we pray for wisdom, knowledge, understanding, right judgement, truth and light –we pray for those discerning God's will in their lives and we pray for those who feel like they have lost Jesus. We especially pray for priests to have the humility to learn from children. And we pray for the grace to always follow the Father's call, regardless of the cost to us and to those who we love on earth.

Sorrowful Mystery of the Rosary

(Tuesday and Friday)

First Mystery: The Agony of Jesus in the Garden

In this mystery, we see how the 'Fiat' of Our Lady in the Annunciation was the same 'Fiat' that Jesus lived all of the days of His life –even in and through death. Our Lady's 'Fiat' drew strength from Christ's Perfect 'Fiat' on the Cross even before He was born (which we see and hear so clearly in the Gospel accounts of the Agony in the Garden). This is because His Fiat was eternal –He was God –and He always lived according to the Perfect Will of the Father regardless of the cost. We see the struggle of His Fiat in His Most Precious Blood sweated from His Heart's battle in Gethsemane –and we see how when His human friends failed Him, the Father Providentially provided strength and comfort to His pain through an angel sent from heaven.

Instinctively Jesus' thoughts in the Garden that night had to have turned to St. Joseph, who never would have abandoned Him (or fallen asleep on Him) as His disciples did. How many sleepless nights did St. Joseph stay awake to watch and pray over Jesus. And his memory – along with the knowledge of His Mother's prayers and love keeping vigil for Him that night –gave Jesus comfort and strength. A rock provided a resting place for Jesus' Agony in the Garden, but in this mystery we pray that it is our hearts –full of love and surrender –that provide a pillow where He can rest here on earth today. We offer this mystery so that we may faithfully say 'Fiat' not only with our tongues, but more deeply with our lives, our blood, sweat and tears, with our faith –along with Jesus in the Garden of Olives all of the days of our lives.

Second Mystery: The Scourging at the Pillar

In this mystery, we see a torrential rain of Christ's love for us, poured out through the shower of His Merciful Blood in the Scourging. The God Who created the heavens and the earth allows Himself to be bound and tortured simply out of love for us. The angels stood in horror to see the torture of the God-Man. This is the first Eucharistic slaughter –the desecration of His Body, Blood, Soul and Divinity –offered as the price of our redemption. Here we bind our wills and hearts to the Sacred Heart of Jesus and we ask for to love in a way worthy of His Gift of Self to us. And we pray for the conversion, healing and miraculous graces that our own lives need, as well as the lives of all of those for whom we pray.

Third Mystery: The Crowning with Thorns

In this mystery, we meditate on how Jesus Christ, the King of kings and Lord of lords –the Maker of Heaven and Earth –is put on trial, accused falsely and judged my man, mocked in His royalty and condemned to die. In this mystery we pray for all of those in authority both physically and spiritually over others. We pray for those on trial, for those falsely accused, for those mocked and persecuted for their faith. We pray that our minds may always be held captive to Christ and His Thoughts and Ways. Scripture says, *'My Thoughts are above your thoughts and My Ways above your ways...'* We ask the Lord Jesus to look upon us with pierced Love and to heal our souls with His glance as He healed Peter and called him to repentance in his denial.

Fourth Mystery: The Carrying of the Cross

In this mystery, Jesus takes up His Cross for us. The Cross in His Heart was heavier than the Cross on His back –and as He carried His load in humble, meek patience and mercy, He left bloody footprints along the way for us to follow Him. *'If anyone would come after me, let him take up his cross and follow me. Those who try to save their life will lose it. But those who lose their life for My sake will save it for eternity.'* In this mystery we see the great compassion that Veronica had for Jesus, that Simon and the weeping women showed to Him along the way. Jesus left His Face's Image on Veronica's veil, but all the more He imprinted His Love within her heart. He called the weeping women to look to the Father and what is most important in life, to lament the sin of their children more than the blood on His back. And He entrusted a great mission to Simon of Cyrene –which was to do all he could to carry the crosses of those weaker than him that he would come to meet during the duration of his life. In this mystery, we pray for the gift of compassion as Our Lady had –feeling in Her Heart the suffering Her Son endured as acutely as if She endured it Herself. And we pray that we may always have the courage to follow the bloody footsteps of Christ and to show compassion to each soul He brings to us along our Calvary way.

Fifth Mystery: The Crucifixion and Death of our Lord

In this mystery, we see the hands that healed, the feet that walked countless miles to save the lost, the face that radiated on Mt. Tabor, the lips that spoke the message of peace, the glance that forgave all sinners –now pierced through with nails, darkened by suffering, dried up by thirst, disfigured by blood and crucified completely on account of our sins. In this mystery we pray in reparation for our sins against Jesus' sacred humanity and divinity. We ask for a fire of divine love to explode from His Heart pouring forth blood and water on Calvary. We ask to share this crucified love with Jesus and so one day merit (because of Him) to bask in heavenly glory praising the Father in the Spirit, with all of the angels and saints forever.

Luminous Mystery of the Rosary

(Thursday)

First Mystery: The Baptism of Jesus in the Jordan

In this mystery we see Jesus descend into the Jordan to be baptized by St. John the Baptist. In this great act of humility we see a God who preaches more by His Life and example than even by His astounding words. In this mystery we pray for the gifts of our own Baptisms to be stirred into flame –so that we can truly live as the children of God that we were created to be. We pray that we can live lives worthy of the Father saying about us as He did Jesus, *'This is my beloved son (or daughter).'* May we truly come to grasp our belovedness to God and to live lives that always respond to this love in full. We also pray for our godchildren, our godparents and for those who have not received the gift of Baptism yet, especially for children who have been left spiritually neglected.

Second Mystery: The Wedding at Cana

In this mystery Our Lady says *'They have no wine,'* and *'Do whatever He tells you.'* In the first line she is presenting our needs to the Lord. She is saying about our lives, too, *'they have no health, they have no finances, they need conversion, they have no peace, they have no hope.'* In this mystery we entrust our prayers to Jesus through the Heart and lips of His Mother. And in the second part of this story we receive not only directions from Our Lady to *'do whatever He tells you,'* but Her words are efficacious in bringing us strength through their instruction. We see here how the faith of Our Lady can touch (and almost change) the Heart of God in His response to us. At first, Jesus says, *'It is not My time...'* but after looking at Her Heart, Her faith and listening to Her Love, the very 'time of God' is changed and great miracles are ushered in.

This changing of water to wine would later be the changing of wine into His Blood in order to save us in the Eucharist and on the Cross. Our Lady did not look at the price Her request of Jesus would cost Her Heart (for by ushering in His public ministry She would have to 'work' through suffering and prayer with Him) –instead She looked for the good of Her children. In this mystery, we entrust all of our lives, our needs, our concerns and problems to the prayerful intercession of Mary. We ask Her to take them to Jesus and we ask Her to pray for us to always know the will of God so that we courageously can 'do whatever He tells us' every day of our lives.

Third Mystery: The Proclamation of the Kingdom
(the Preaching of Jesus, the Call to Repentance and the Healing Miracles)

In this mystery, we see the essence of the missionary work of Jesus. We meditate on His preaching, on His gift of forgiveness of sins and on the many ways that He healed (and delivered) both bodies and souls who encountered Him. In this mystery, we pray especially for missionaries who bring hope through their words to the broken-hearted, who bring light to those lost in darkness, who speak words that soften hearts hardened in sin and who inspire with a fire of love and holy zeal all who encounter them. We pray for priests to have the Heart of the Savior in their interactions with souls, especially in the confessional. We pray for a true knowledge of and repentance for our own sins, and for the gift of forgiveness of those who sin against us. And we pray for healing for all those who are sick, for those who we love, and for those who have no one else to remember them in prayer before the throne of God. We pray for spiritual protection and fruitfulness in all missionary work and for the Lord to provide for the needs of missionaries everywhere. We ask this in the name of Jesus Christ, our Lord.

Fourth Mystery: The Transfiguration

In this mystery we remember the times of great grace that God gives to strengthen us before He lays the cross on our shoulders and within our hearts. In the transfiguration, Peter, James and John experienced divine awesomeness as they watched Jesus discuss His upcoming passion and death with Moses and Elijah. Even today, God gives great gifts of divine favor to us (sometimes they are recognized by us and sometimes they are not) to strengthen us for the tasks He also entrusts to our lives. We remember in thanksgiving the great graces of Our Lady appearing to us over the years to shower us with Her Motherly Love. We especially remember in Fatima where She asks us to pray for the conversion of Russia and for the Triumph of Her Immaculate Heart, which will come at the cost of many motherly tears. We pray for Her intentions and we join our sacrifices and sufferings to this prayer so that She may conform us to Christ.

<u>Fifth Mystery:</u> The Institution of the Eucharist as a Foreshadowing of the Cross

In this mystery, we meditate on the greatest gift that Jesus left with us –being His very Own Body, Blood, Soul and Divinity in the Eucharist. He said, *'This is My Body. This is My Blood. Which will be shed for you. Do this in remembrance of Me.'* Jesus wants us to remember His Passion so that we recognize His Love gifted to us in the Eucharistic Host. The gift of His Heart in this way had a price –it cost Him everything offered back to the Father. In this mystery, let us pray for a healing of indifference in the world (and Church) to Jesus' Presence in the Eucharist. Let us pray for a greater love, reverence and devotion to His Eucharistic Heart and Blood. Let us pray that as we receive Him into our own bodies and hearts to be a tabernacle of His Presence in the world, that we may be conformed into and image of Him in the world. And let us pray that Eucharistic adoration may be central in our lives and in each parish, at each shrine, in each house of prayer and in each city of the world. May the Eucharist be our lamp, our blanket, our medicine and the source and summit of our love.

Glorious Mystery of the Rosary
(Wednesday and Sunday)

First Mystery: The Resurrection of Jesus Christ

In this mystery, we bring to Jesus each one of our lives' wounds suffered in union with His Bloody Martyrdom on the Cross –and we ask Him to heal them, transform them, fill them with new life, new beauty, new meaning –and to resurrect them in full. So often in life we are like Mary Magdalene –standing face to Face with Jesus, and yet not recognizing Him because we are focusing more on our own tears then on His Love. And He calls our name as He called Mary's name –and in that voice knowing us and calling us by name, saying 'You are Mine' we are made whole. We ask Jesus to put miraculous resurrected grace within each of our needs and wounds. We pray for peace and joy, no matter what we encounter in life. And we praise and thank Him for the marvelous, transforming power of His Love.

Second Mystery: The Ascension of Jesus to Heaven

In this mystery, we meditate on the mystery of attentive waiting for the Lord. In this mystery, the world was still up in arms over Jesus' Passion, Death and Resurrection. The Apostles had been given a job and yet did not yet have the fullness of grace that would come in the gift of the Holy Spirit at Pentecost to do all that the Father would ask of them. And so in this mystery they had to live trust and in a state of active, patient waiting. It was a prayerful stance of expectation –full of hope –that they had to keep their hearts waiting in. God was stretching their hearts in this time so that they could receive the fullness of the Holy Spirit when He came. And they had to do this obedient waiting of preparatory prayer with Our Lady leading them. In this mystery, we, too, pray for the gift of patience, of hope, of trust, and of exercising faith –in order that our hearts are expanded wide enough to receive the fullness of God's gifts. Amen.

<u>Third Mystery:</u> The Descent of the Holy Spirit upon the Apostles at Pentecost

In this mystery we meditate on the explosion of the Holy Spirit's Love that took place within the hearts of the Apostles and disciples o Pentecost. We remember that although the Holy Spirit came in a strong wind, with powerful fire and charismatic gifts at that first Pentecost, He doesn't always come into our lives with a 'boom and a bang'. Mary and Joseph were more full of the Holy Spirit than we ever could be, and He filled them gently, silently, hiddenly in all that they thought, said and did –and yet His

Presence was ever steadfast, sure and faithfully strong. In this mystery, we ask for the Holy Spirit to fill us as completely as He filled the hearts of Jesus, Mary and Joseph. And we ask for all of His gifts, fruits, graces, virtues and charisms so that we can live authentic holiness and become the great unique saints that He created us to be.

Fourth Mystery: The Assumption of Mary into Heaven

In this mystery, we remember that the foundation of Mary's assumption was Her holiness. And Our Lady was full of grace and holiness primarily because the depth of Her humility and purity allowed room for God to enter into Her to dwell in full. In this mystery, we pray for those two graces of authentic humility and purity (of mind, body, heart, soul and intention). We ask that through these graces, God's Divine Love may enter in to make us entirely one with Him.

Fifth Mystery: The Coronation of Mary as Queen of Heaven and Earth

In this mystery, we consecrate ourselves again to the Immaculate and Sorrowful Heart of Our Heavenly Mother. She is our Queen. We consecrate to Her our minds, bodies, hearts, souls, spirits, personalities, emotions, memories, families, relationships, work, ministry, homes, finances, possessions, vocation –all that we have and all that we are – for her to use at Her will for the greatest glory of God the Father. Amen.

Mary Kloska's Vocation

For more information about Mary Kloska's vocation, books, icons (Artist Shop), music, podcasts, prayer ministry or to become a monthly donor to support her missionary work, please see:

www.marykloskafiat.com

Blog: http://fiatlove.blogspot.com

Books:

The Holiness of Womanhood:
https://enroutebooksandmedia.com/holinessofwomanhood/

Out of the Darkness:
https://enroutebooksandmedia.com/outofthedarkness/

In Our Lady's Shadow:

The Spirituality of Praying for Priests:

https://enroutebooksandmedia.com/shadow/

A Heart Frozen in the Wilderness: Reflections of a Siberian Missionary:

https://enroutebooksandmedia.com/frozen/

La Santidad de La Mujer:

https://enroutebooksandmedia.com/lasantidaddelamujer/

Swietosc Kobiecosci:

https://enroutebooksandmedia.com/swietosckobiecosci/

Z Ciemnosci:

Z ciemności… | En Route Books and Media

Fuera de las Tinieblas:

https://enroutebooksandmedia.com/fueradelastinieblas/

Radio

Podcasts: https://wcatradio.com/heartoffiatcrucifiedlove/

YouTube VIDEO Podcasts

Playlist: http://www.tinyurl.com/marykloska

Artist Shop (Icon prints and other items for sale): http://marykloskafiat.threadless.com

Music CD "FIAT" is also available on all music platforms.

Patreon: www.patreon.com/marykloskafiat

Made in the USA
Middletown, DE
25 September 2021